Interviewing as Qualitative Research

A Guide for Researchers in Education and the Social Sciences

Third Edition

Interviewing as Qualitative Research

A Guide for Researchers in Education and the Social Sciences

Third Edition

Irving Seidman

TEACHERS COLLEGE PRESS

Teachers College, Columbia University
New York and London

Published by Teachers College Press, 1234 Amsterdam Avenue, New York, NY 10027

Library of Congress Cataloging-in-Publication Data

Seidman, Irving, 1937–
   Interviewing as qualitative research : a guide for researchers in education and the social sciences / Irving Seidman.–3rd ed.
     p. cm.
   Includes bibliographical references and index.
   ISBN-13: 978-0-8077-4666-0 (alk. paper)
   ISBN-10: 0-8077-4666-5 (alk. paper)
   1. Interviewing. 2. Social sciences–Research–Methodology. 3. Education–Research–Methodology. I. Title.

   H61.28.S45 2005
   300'.72'3–dc22   2005053816

ISBN-13 978-0-8077-4666-0 (paper)   ISBN-10 0-8077-4666-5 (paper)

Printed on acid-free paper
Manufactured in the United States of America

13   12   11   10   09   08   07   8   7   6   5   4   3

Contents

Preface

In my experience as a teacher, I have worked with many graduate students who have deep and passionate interests they wish to pursue in their dissertations. Often, however, they are stymied by the lack of an appropriate and feasible methodology. They are, in Sartre's (1968) terms, "in search of a method."

This book is intended for doctoral candidates who are engaged in that search and who think that in-depth interviewing might be appropriate for them and their research topic. It will also serve more experienced researchers who are interested in qualitative research and may be turning to the possibilities of interviewing for the first time. Finally, the book is geared to professors in search of a supplementary text on in-depth interviewing that connects method and technique with broader issues of qualitative research. For both individual and classroom use, the book provides a step-by-step introduction to the research process using in-depth interviewing and places those steps within the context of significant issues in qualitative research.

The text centers on a phenomenological approach to in-depth interviewing. The Introduction outlines how I came to do interviewing research. Chapter 1 discusses a rationale for using interviewing as a research method and the potential of narratives as ways of knowing. Chapter 2 presents a structure for in-depth, phenomenologically based interviewing that my associates and I have used in our research projects. The text provides specific guidance on how to carry out this approach to interviewing and the principles of adapting it to one's own goals. Chapter 3 explores issues that may make proposal writing daunting and discusses meaningful but simple questions that can guide the researcher through the process. Chapter 4 stresses pitfalls and snares to avoid in the process, and discusses issues in establishing access to, making contact with, and selecting participants. Chapter 5, responding to the increasing concern about ethical issues in interviewing research, introduces the Institutional Review Board (IRB) process and its implications for researchers who interview. This chapter explains the risks inherent in interviewing research that lead IRBs to require Informed Consent Forms. The chapter explicates the major points that an informed consent form should include, alerts readers to corresponding ethical issues, and assesses the complexities and debates that swirl around the IRB process and informed consent. Chapter 6 avoids a cookbook approach but discusses specific interviewing skills and techniques and links them to important issues in interviewing and qualitative research. The chapter stresses how to listen as well as how to ask questions. Chapter 7 explores interviewing as a relationship. It places that relationship within the context of major contemporary social issues that are often embedded in the interaction between interviewers and participants. The chapter also faces squarely the potential for confusing in-depth interviewing research with therapy, cautions readers about the complexities of rapport, and stresses equity as the necessary element in interviewing relationships. Chapter 8 discusses how to manage, work with, and share the data generated by in-depth interviewing. It guides the reader through a step-by-step process of working with the extensive material that interviewers gather. The chapter presents two potential analytic processes: one leading to identifying themes that emerge from the interviewing material and the other leading to developing narrative profiles of participants' experiences and the meaning they make of those experiences. Both are ways of sharing and discussing results of interviewing with a wider audience.

The Appendix presents two narrative profiles. These examples reveal the potential of interviewing both to tap the depth of life-and-death experiences and to explore the complexities and significances of everyday experience.

While proposing a phenomenological approach to in-depth interviewing, the book provides and discusses principles and methods that can be adapted to a range of interviewing approaches. Throughout the text I have provided examples from interviews done by colleagues, graduate students with whom I work, and from my own research that illustrate the issues under discussion. I try to maintain a balance between sharing my experience with in-depth interviewing so that a reader can use what he or she may, and giving enough explicit guidance so that a reader can successfully conceptualize and carry out a research project based on the approach described.

In addition, I describe a practice project that individuals, entire classes, or workshops can use to gain concrete experience with the method in a short amount of time. I also guide readers to ways to study, reflect upon, and assess their own interviewing practice.

My goal has been to write a text clear and practical enough to provide useful guidance about in-depth interviewing as a research method. At the same time my objective has been to connect that method to broader issues in qualitative research. To that end, I selectively refer readers to additional readings that lead to further consideration of methodological, ethical, and philosophical issues in interviewing and qualitative research. In addition, the Internet has become an important research tool, and I have pointed readers to relevant Internet resources that are now readily available. My hope is that the emphasis on principles in the guidance the book offers and the integration of broader issues in qualitative research will make the book useful to a wide range of researchers in education and the social sciences.

Aristotle (1976) said that virtuous and ethical behavior involves doing well, whatever we do. My further hope is that this book will guide interviewing researchers to a method that engages their minds, touches their hearts, and supports their doing good work.

Acknowledgments

One of the pleasures for me in the years since this book was first published has been the contact I have had with new researchers who have e-mailed and called to discuss their research projects. Some of their names appear in Chapter 2. To all of them I express my appreciation for their interest in and work with the approach to research outlined in this book.

I am indebted to Ms. Julie Simpson, Manager of Research Conduct and Compliance Services of the Office of Sponsored Research and Service, University of New Hampshire, Durham. Throughout my exploration of the Institutional Review Board review process, Ms. Simpson has guided me on specific and general issues. While she is not responsible for any shortcomings in this area, her generous, informed, and thoughtful guidance led me to a better understanding of the IRB process.

Thank you to Margaret Burggren, Richard Clark, Atron Gentry, Farshid Hajir, Anne Herrington, Robert Maloy, Gareth Matthews, Heidi McKee, Barbara Morgan, and Robert Zussman, present and former colleagues and associates at the University of Massachusetts, Amherst; to Larry Ludlow and Gerald Pine of Boston College; and Linda Shopes of the American Historical Association. Each offered me important direct or indirect support in this effort.

Throughout this work—thanks to the support of Linda Griffin, Ken Divoll, and my colleagues in the Secondary Teacher Education Program—I have had the research assistance of Frederick Asante-Somuah, an outstanding graduate student from Ghana. He has been meticulous in his efforts, good spirited, and talented in his command of the new electronic databases in our library. Thanks also to Linda Neas and Jennifer Goodheart for their timely support. I also wish to express my appreciation to the Interlibrary Loan Department, and to Stephen McGinty and Barbara Morgan, Reference Librarians of our W.E.B. Du Bois Library.

I am deeply appreciative of the efforts of doctoral candidates Tony Burgess and Nate Allen of George Washington University and Margaret Boyko, Roel Garcia, and Tom Telicki of the School of Education, University of Massachusetts, Amherst who read and gave me specific, thoughtful, and very useful feedback to Chapter 5.

My wife, Linda, and son, Ethan, have once again contributed significantly to whatever strengths the book may have through their considered and talented editing.

Thank you to David Schwandt and Margaret Gorman of the Executive Leadership Program of George Washington University and to the officers of the New England Educational Research Organization (NEERO) who have offered me opportunities to present workshops on in-depth interviewing in which I have been able to clarify and test ideas in this book. I also want to express my continued gratitude to Daniel P. Schwartz for his teaching, which stays with me.

I deeply appreciate Teachers College Press's support of this third edition and in particular the thoughtfulness of Jessica Balun, Susan Liddicoat, Nancy Power, Peter Sieger, and Shannon Waite.

While the above acknowledgment focuses on those to whom I am indebted for their support of this third edition, I do not want the publishing of a new edition of this book to mean the loss of attribution to family, friends, teachers, colleagues, associates, and graduate students whose early support has stayed with me as I have continued this work: Clifford Adelman, Theresa Barton, Sara Biondello, John Booss, Kathryn Charmaz, Richard Clark, Elizabeth Cohen, William Compagnone, Edward. W. Hughes Jr., Sarah Kuhn, Alice Levenson, Ruth Levenson, Sari and George Lipkin, Lawrence F. Locke, Robert Maloy, Lori Mestre, Linda Miller-Cleary, Judith H. Miller, Jane Nagle, James O'Donnell, Sally Rubinstein, Mary Bray Schatzkamer, Alex Seidman, Louis Seidman, Rachel Filene Seidman, Patricio Sullivan, Mark Tetrault, and John Wirt.

Since the last edition of this book, our daughter Rachel and son-in-law Benjamin Filene have brought into the world another avid listener to stories, their daughter Hazel, younger sister of Eliza. When asked what it meant to live well, Freud was reported to have said, "To work and love well." In my continued and certainly imperfect attempt to merge the two, I dedicate this edition to our granddaughter, Hazel.

Introduction

How I Came to Interviewing

In my study at home, I have a picture of my grandfather, whom I never met, on the bookshelf. He was born sometime around 1870 and he died in the early 1940s. In the sepia photograph that I have, he is a bearded man with sad eyes, wearing a worn jacket over a sweater and tie. His eyes look out at me no matter where I am in the room.

Whenever I asked my father about his father, he said his father was a religious man. "What did he do?" I would ask, and my father would say, "He studied." I never got very much of his story. I know only that he was a religious man, that he studied, that he didn't do much else, that his family was poor, and that he died of a heart attack running away from the Germans early in World War II.

My father was an immigrant from Russia. He came to this country with my mother in 1921. While I was growing up in Cleveland, Ohio, and upon visits to my family home later, I asked my father about his experiences in Russia (my mother, also from Russia, died in 1963): What was it like to live there? How did he come to leave? I asked him about his family, about what it was like to be a child in Russia.

His reply, almost invariably, was, "Why do you want to know? We were poor. Everyone was poor. There was nothing there. America is wonderful. Why do you want to know about Russia?" My father died in 1989 and, although I have accumulated a few anecdotes about his days in Russia, I did not learn the story of his life there, and I never will.

After graduating from college, I earned an M.A.T. degree and taught English for 4½ years in every grade from 7 through 12. Perhaps it was as a teacher of English that I first came to see stories and the details of people's lives as a way of knowing and understanding.

To suggest that stories are a way to knowledge and understanding may not seem scholarly. When I was earning my doctorate in education in the mid-1960s, the faculty in my graduate program in teacher education seemed almost totally committed to building knowledge in education through experimentation. My graduate experience was governed by a sense that research in education could be as scientific as it was in the natural and

1

physical sciences. Experimentalists informed by behaviorism dominated my graduate experience in research. I remember sitting in an advanced educational psychology class. The professor was discussing conditioning as a basis for understanding learning. It was a class of about 60, but discussion was officially encouraged. I raised my hand and said something about humans being different from rats because people had language. I don't remember exactly what the professor said in return, but it was not what I would call today a collaborative response.

That day brought to a culmination my feeling of being stifled and frustrated by behaviorism during the first year of my graduate study. Only of late have I come to appreciate a suggestion my doctoral advisor and mentor, Alfred Grommon, made to me: that I do a biography of one of the early presidents of the National Council of Teachers of English for my dissertation. At that time, I considered his suggestion well intended but somehow not connected to my interests. Now I realize that he may have been offering me a way out of the Procrustean bed of behaviorism and experimentalism that pervaded my graduate experience.

Despite my aversions, I did an experimental dissertation. I designed a study of the effects on students' achievement motivation of teachers' comments on their writing. I had different treatment groups; I established independent variables and dependent variables; I enlisted a group of English teachers in the field to carry out "the treatments" that I had designed on "the subjects."

Nathan Gage's (1963) *Handbook of Research on Teaching* had recently been published. In some respects it was treated as a bible in our graduate program. I remember reading and rereading, and developing mnemonic codes to help me remember the threats to validity and reliability described and analyzed in Campbell and Stanley's (1963) chapter on "Experimental and Quasi-Experimental Design for Research in Teaching."

While at the time I chafed under the heavy emphasis on experimentalism, I now respect how committed my graduate institution was to research in education. Despite my resistance to the approach then, I now realize how valuable and important it was for me to confront the assumptions of positivism and behaviorism that seemed to me to dominate the institution. In my thinking about both teaching and research, my professional career has been shaped by that confrontation. There were also, at the time, professors who provided an alternative point of view. They helped open my mind to exploring new intellectual paths, especially the impact of social and cultural forces on individual experience in education. In the end, my graduate school communicated a sense of imperative about research in education that has had a long-lasting effect on me for which I am grateful.

As I continued my career in education after I earned my doctorate in 1967, I took a position that left me confused about research. I joined the English Department of the University of Washington as one of three faculty members in English education. I had surprisingly little contact with the College of Education as I began to face the pressures of publishing in my field. On some levels, I was estranged from my own dissertation because I had not really believed in its methodology, so I did not then and never have sought to publish an article based on it. That first and formative year, I did do some writing, but no research. I often wonder how I would have figured out my relationship to research if I had stayed at the University of Washington. Given my experimental experience, my discomfort with it, and my position as a teacher educator in a strong, conservative English department where the notion of research was that of literary scholarship, my research options at that time were not clear to me.

I stayed at the University of Washington only a year. I had a good position in an exceptionally strong department in a public university that was the pride of the Northwest; but I left in 1968 to become the assistant dean of the School of Education at the University of Massachusetts at Amherst under the leadership of Dwight Allen. This is not the place to dwell at length on that part of the story (*Frenzy at UMass*, 1970; Resnik, 1972). It looms larger in my mind, I am sure, than in most others'. Suffice it to say that our goal reflected the times and our sense of them. Our objective was to reform professional education and to have our School of Education play a role in making society more equitable. I will always respect the idealism of those goals. In our inexperience and naiveté, we made many mistakes along the way—in and among some significant accomplishments. As the times changed, and our mistakes accumulated, a new administration was called for. I was a faculty member again after 6 intense years as an administrator. Although I learned much about higher education during my tenure as an administrator, I gained little new experience in doing research.

After my administrative years, I was fortunate enough to take a sabbatical in London with my family. I had the chance to do reading that would allow me to return responsibly to my teaching. In addition to reading works on the teaching of English, which I had been away from for 7 years, I read Thomas Kuhn's (1970) *The Structure of Scientific Revolution* and thought about my experience with science and research as a graduate student. I read that book just in time. When I got back to the States, references to "governing paradigms" in journal articles abounded.

Upon my return, I co-taught a course with Robert Woodbury on Leadership in Higher Education. A new faculty member by the name of David Schuman had joined our school in the area of higher education. Through my teaching in the Higher Education Program I came to know him. Of the many constitutive events that led me to interviewing as a research methodology, meeting and working with Schuman was the most significant. Because I had rejected the approach to research I had learned in graduate school and had not learned a new approach in my short time at Washington, or in the 6 years I was an administrator, I was, paradoxically, a relatively experienced faculty member searching for a research methodology.

Schuman was beginning to write a book based on interviewing research that he had done with Kenneth Dolbeare. Schuman's book *Policy Analysis, Education, and Everyday Life* did not come out until 1982, but in the meantime he generously shared with Patrick Sullivan and me his methodological approach, which he called "phenomenological interviewing." He also directed me to some of the readings he had done in coming to the type of interviewing research he and Dolbeare had done. I remember in particular his suggesting to me that I read William James's (1947) *Essays in Radical Empiricism* and *In a Pluralistic Universe*, Sartre's (1968) *Search for a Method*, Matson's (1966) *The Broken Image*, and, most directly relevant, Alfred Schutz's (1967) *The Phenomenology of the Social World*.

I was ready for what Schuman was generously willing to share. I remember the feeling that I would like to do interviewing as a research method. I remember thinking what a good way it was to learn about people and schools as I listened to Schuman and began to build in my mind upon what he was saying. Additionally, I had had experience with psychotherapy. Through that process, I learned to appreciate even further the importance of language and stories in a person's life as ways toward knowing and understanding. That personal experience made me even more ready to consider interviewing as a research method.

Sullivan and I were co-teaching a course for community college teachers on critical issues in community college teaching. Sullivan, with his colleague, Judithe Speidel, had earlier done a documentary film on the Shakers (*The Shaker Legacy*, 1976), and we decided now to do a film on teaching in community colleges based on the interviewing method we had learned from Schuman. We received a grant from the Exxon Corporation to support our interviewing 25 community college teachers on how they came to teaching, what it was like for them, and what it meant to them.

The film was produced in 1982, and we then received a second grant from the National Institute of Education (NIE) to expand our interviewing to community college faculty in California and New York. The work continued to be a deeply satisfying way to do research. I loved talking with people about their work as faculty members and learning about community college education through the experience of those who taught there. We interviewed a total of 76 community college faculty and, through the efforts of Mary Bray Schatzkamer, 24 students to try to gain an understanding of what it was like to work and teach in a community college. That interviewing led to a draft of a manuscript called "What We Have Learned About In-Depth Interviewing" that was published as Chapter 14 of our Final Report to NIE (Seidman, Sullivan, & Schatzkamer, 1983) and a book on community college teaching called *In the Words of the Faculty* (Seidman, 1985).

While doing our research on community college faculty, Sullivan and I began to co-teach a graduate seminar, In-Depth Interviewing and Issues in Qualitative Work. I continue to teach that seminar and to do interviewing research.

Interviewing the community college teachers was the first research I had done that was neither literary nor experimental. I had finally found a way to do "empirical" work that was emotionally and intellectually satisfying. In spite of problems and complications everywhere in the research process, from conceiving the idea and contacting participants to writing up the results of 3 years of interviewing, this kind of work was and continues to be deeply satisfying for me. It is hard and sometimes draining, but I have never lost the feeling that it is a privilege to gather the stories of people through interviewing and to come to understand their experience through their stories. Sharing those stories through developing profiles of the people I had interviewed in their own words and making thematic connections among their experiences proved to be a fruitful way of working with the material and of writing about what I had learned. A good deal of what follows is an attempt to describe and explain the roots of the intellectual and emotional pleasure I have gained from interviewing as a research method in education.

One final introductory note: Although this book concentrates on in-depth interviewing as a method of research in education, I am not proposing it as the sole, or the best, method of doing research. Some scholars argue that having multiple sources of data is one of the intrinsic characteristics of qualitative research (see Patton, 1989). The interviewing method I describe, explain, and, I hope, illuminate can be done in combination with other approaches to understanding the world outside ourselves. On the other hand, I think a case can be made that in some research situations the in-depth interview, as the primary and perhaps singular method of investigation, is most appropriate. Use of in-depth interviews alone, when done with skill, can avoid tensions that sometimes arise when a researcher uses multiple methods. That is especially the case when those methods may be based on different assumptions of what it means to understand the experience of others.

Chapter 1

Why Interview?

I interview because I am interested in other people's stories. Most simply put, stories are a way of knowing. The root of the word *story* is the Greek word *histor*, which means one who is "wise" and "learned" (Watkins, 1985, p. 74). Telling stories is essentially a meaning-making process. When people tell stories, they select details of their experience from their stream of consciousness. Every whole story, Aristotle tells us, has a beginning, a middle, and an end (Butcher, 1902). In order to give the details of their experience a beginning, middle, and end, people must reflect on their experience. It is this process of selecting constitutive details of experience, reflecting on them, giving them order, and thereby making sense of them that makes telling stories a meaning-making experience. (See Schutz, 1967, p. 12 and p. 50, for aspects of the relationship between reflection and meaning making.)

Every word that people use in telling their stories is a microcosm of their consciousness (Vygotsky, 1987, pp. 236–237). Individuals' consciousness gives access to the most complicated social and educational issues, because social and educational issues are abstractions based on the concrete experience of people. W. E. B. Du Bois knew this when he wrote, "I seem to see a way of elucidating the inner meaning of life and significance of that race problem by explaining it in terms of the one human life that I know best" (Wideman, 1990, p. xiv).

Although anthropologists have long been interested in people's stories as a way of understanding their culture, such an approach to research in education has not been widely accepted. For many years those who were trying to make education a respected academic discipline in universities argued that education could be a science (Bailyn, 1963). They urged their colleagues in education to adapt research models patterned after those in the natural and physical sciences.

In the 1970s a reaction to the dominance of experimental, quantitative, and behaviorist research in education began to develop (Gage, 1989). The critique had its own energy and was also a reflection of the era's more general resistance to received authority (Gitlin, 1987, esp.

chap. 4). Researchers in education split into two, almost warring, camps: quantitative and qualitative.

It is interesting to note that the debate between the two camps got especially fierce and the polemics more extreme when the economics of higher education took a downturn in the mid-1970s and early 1980s (Gage, 1989). But the political battles were informed by real epistemological differences. The underlying assumptions about the nature of reality, the relationship of the knower and the known, the possibility of objectivity, the possibility of generalization, inherent in each approach are different and to a considerable degree contradictory. To begin to understand these basic differences in assumptions, I urge you to read James (1947), Lincoln and Guba (1985, chap. 1), Mannheim (1975), and Polanyi (1958).

For those interested in interviewing as a method of research, perhaps the most telling argument between the two camps centers on the significance of language to inquiry with human beings. Bertaux (1981) has argued that those who urge educational researchers to imitate the natural sciences seem to ignore one basic difference between the subjects of inquiry in the natural sciences and those in the social sciences: The subjects of inquiry in the social sciences can talk and think. Unlike a planet, or a chemical, or a lever, "If given a chance to talk freely, people appear to know a lot about what is going on" (p. 39).

At the very heart of what it means to be human is the ability of people to symbolize their experience through language. To understand human behavior means to understand the use of language (Heron, 1981). Heron points out that the original and archetypal paradigm of human inquiry is two persons talking and asking questions of each other. He says:

> The use of language, itself, . . . contains within it the paradigm of cooperative inquiry; and since language is the primary tool whose use enables human construing and intending to occur, it is difficult to see how there can be any more fundamental mode of inquiry for human beings into the human condition. (p. 26)

Interviewing, then, is a basic mode of inquiry. Recounting narratives of experience has been the major way throughout recorded history that humans have made sense of their experience. To those who would ask, however, "Is telling stories science?" Peter Reason (1981) would respond,

> The best stories are those which stir people's minds, hearts, and souls and by so doing give them new insights into themselves, their problems and their human condition. The challenge is to develop a human science

that can more fully serve this aim. The question, then, is not "Is story telling science?" but "Can science learn to tell good stories?" (p. 50)

THE PURPOSE OF INTERVIEWING

The purpose of in-depth interviewing is not to get answers to questions, nor to test hypotheses, and not to "evaluate" as the term is normally used. (See Patton, 1989, for an exception.) At the root of in-depth interviewing is an interest in understanding the lived experience of other people and the meaning they make of that experience. (For a deeply thoughtful elaboration of a phenomenological approach to research, see Van Manen, 1990, from whom the notion of exploring "lived" experience mentioned throughout this text is taken.)

Being interested in others is the key to some of the basic assumptions underlying interviewing technique. It requires that we interviewers keep our egos in check. It requires that we realize we are not the center of the world. It demands that our actions as interviewers indicate that others' stories are important.

At the heart of interviewing research is an interest in other individuals' stories because they are of worth. That is why people whom we interview are hard to code with numbers, and why finding pseudonyms for participants[1] is a complex and sensitive task. (See Kvale, 1996, pp. 259–260, for a discussion of the dangers of the careless use of pseudonyms.) Their stories defy the anonymity of a number and almost that of a pseudonym. To hold the conviction that we know enough already and don't need to know others' stories is not only anti-intellectual; it also leaves us, at one extreme, prone to violence to others (Todorov, 1984).

Schutz (1967, chap. 3) offers us guidance. First of all, he says that it is never possible to understand another perfectly, because to do so would mean that we had entered into the other's stream of consciousness and experienced what he or she had. If we could do that, we would *be* that other person.

Recognizing the limits on our understanding of others, we can still strive to comprehend them by understanding their actions. Schutz gives the example of walking in the woods and seeing a man chopping wood. The observer can watch this behavior and have an "observational understanding" of the woodchopper. But what the observer understands as a result of this observation may not be at all consistent with how the woodchopper views his own behavior. (In analogous terms, think of the problem of observing students or teachers.) To understand the woodchopper's behavior, the observer would have to gain access to the woodchopper's "subjective understanding," that is, know what meaning he himself made out of his chopping wood. The way to meaning, Schutz says, is to be able to put behavior in context. Was the woodchopper chopping wood to supply a logger, heat his home, or get in shape? (For Schutz's complete and detailed explication of this argument, see esp. chaps. 1–3. For a thoughtful secondary source on research methodology based on phenomenology, for which Schutz is one primary resource, see Moustakas, 1994.)

Interviewing provides access to the context of people's behavior and thereby provides a way for researchers to understand the meaning of that behavior. A basic assumption in in-depth interviewing research is that the meaning people make of their experience affects the way they carry out that experience (Blumer, 1969, p. 2). To observe a teacher, student, principal, or counselor provides access to their behavior. Interviewing allows us to put behavior in context and provides access to understanding their action. The best article I have read on the importance of context for meaning is Elliot Mishler's (1979) "Meaning in Context: Is There Any Other Kind?" the theme of which was later expanded into his book, *Research Interviewing: Context and Narrative* (1986). Ian Dey (1993) also stresses the significance of context in the interpretation of data in his useful book on qualitative data analysis.

INTERVIEWING: "THE" METHOD OR "A" METHOD?

The primary way a researcher can investigate an educational organization, institution, or process is through the experience of the individual people, the "others" who make up the organization or carry out the process. Social abstractions like "education" are best understood through the experiences of the individuals whose work and lives are the stuff upon which the abstractions are built (Ferrarotti, 1981). So much research is done on schooling in the United States; yet so little of it is based on studies involving the perspective of the students, teachers, administrators, counselors, special subject teachers, nurses, psychologists, cafeteria workers, secretaries, school crossing guards, bus drivers, parents, and school committee members, whose individual and collective experience constitutes schooling.

A researcher can approach the experience of people in contemporary organizations through examining personal and institutional documents, through observation, through exploring history, through experimentation, through questionnaires and surveys, and through a review of existing literature. If the researcher's goal, however, is to understand the meaning people involved in education make of their experience, then interviewing provides a necessary, if not always completely sufficient, avenue of inquiry.

An educational researcher might suggest that the other avenues of inquiry listed above offer access to people's experience and the meaning they make of it as effectively as and at less cost than does interviewing. I would not argue that there is one right way, or that one way is better than another. Howard Becker, Blanche Geer, and Martin Trow carried on an argument in 1957 that still gains attention in the literature because, among other reasons, Becker and Geer seemed to be arguing that participant observation was the single and best way to gather data about people in society. Trow took exception and argued back that for some purposes interviewing is far superior (Becker & Geer, 1957; Trow, 1957).

The adequacy of a research method depends on the purpose of the research and the questions being asked (Locke, 1989). If a researcher is asking a question such as, "How do people behave in this classroom?" then participant observation might be the best method of inquiry. If the researcher is asking, "How does the placement of students in a level of the tracking system correlate with social class and race?" then a survey may be the best approach. If the researcher is wondering whether a new curriculum affects students' achievements on standardized tests, then a quasi-experimental, controlled study might be most effective. Research interests don't always or often come out so neatly. In many cases, research interests have many levels, and as a result multiple methods may be appropriate. If the researcher is interested, however, in what it is like for students to be in the classroom, what their experience is, and what meaning they make out of that experience—if the interest is in what Schutz (1967) calls their "subjective understanding"—then it seems to me that interviewing, in most cases, may be the best avenue of inquiry.

I say "in most cases," because below a certain age, interviewing children may not work. I would not rule out the possibility, however, of sitting down with even very young children to ask them about their experience. Carlisle (1988) interviewed first-grade students about their responses to literature. She found that although she had to shorten the length of time that she interviewed students, she was successful at exploring with first graders their experience with books.

WHY NOT INTERVIEW?

Interviewing research takes a great deal of time and, sometimes, money. The researcher has to conceptualize the project, establish access and make contact with participants, interview them, transcribe the data, and then work with the material and share what he or she has learned. Sometimes I sense that a new researcher is choosing one method because he or she thinks it will be easier than another. Any method of inquiry worth anything takes time, thoughtfulness, energy, and money. But interviewing is especially labor intensive. If the researcher does not have the money or the support to hire secretarial help to transcribe tapes, it is his or her labor that is at stake. (See Chapter 8.)

Interviewing requires that researchers establish access to, and make contact with, potential participants whom they have never met. If they are unduly shy about themselves or hate to make phone calls, the process of getting started can be daunting. On the other hand, overcoming shyness, taking the initiative, establishing contact, and scheduling and completing the first set of interviews can be a very satisfying accomplishment.

My sense is that graduate programs today in general, and the one in which I teach in particular, are much more individualized and less monolithic than I thought them to be when I was a doctoral candidate. Students have a choice of the type of research methodology they wish to pursue. But in some graduate programs there may be a cost to pay for that freedom: Those interested in qualitative research may not be required to learn the tenets of what is called "quantitative" research. As a result, some students tend not to understand the history of the method they are using or the critique of positivism and experimentalism out of which some approaches to qualitative research in education grew. (For those interested in learning that critique as an underpinning for their work, as a start see Johnson, 1975; Lincoln & Guba, 1985.)

Graduate candidates must understand the so-called paradigm wars (Gage, 1989) that took place in the 1970s and 1980s and are still being waged in the 2000s (Shavelson & Towne, 2002). By not being aware of the history of the battle and the fields upon which it has been fought, students may not understand their own position in it and the potential implications for their career as it continues. If doctoral candidates choose to use interviewing as a research methodology for their dissertation or other early research, they should know that their choice to do qualitative research has not been the dominant one in the history of educational research. Although qualitative research has gained ground in the last 30 years, professional organizations, some journals in education, and personnel committees on which senior faculty tend to sit, are often dominated by those who have a predilection for quantitative research. Furthermore, the federal government issued an additional challenge to qualitative researchers when it enacted legislation that guides federal funding agencies to award grants to researchers whose methodologies adhere to "scientific" standards. (See the definition of "scientific" in section 102,18 of the Education Sciences Reform Act of 2002.) In some arenas, doctoral candidates choosing to do qualitative rather than quantitative research may have to fight a stiffer battle to establish themselves as credible. They may also have to be comfortable with being outside the center of the conventional educational establishments. They will have to learn to search out funding agencies, journals, and publishers open to qualitative approaches. (For a discussion of some of these issues, see Mishler, 1986, esp. pp. 141–143; Wolcott, 1994, pp. 417–422.)

Although the choice of a research method ideally is determined by what one is trying to learn, those coming into the field of educational research must know that some researchers and scholars see the choice as a political and moral one. (See Bertaux, 1981; Fay, 1987; Gage, 1989; Lather, 1986a, 1986b; Popkowitz, 1984.) Those who espouse qualitative research often take the high moral road. Among other criticism, they decry the way quantitative research turns human beings into numbers.

But, there are equally serious moral issues involved in qualitative research. As I read Todorov's (1984) *The Conquest of America,* I began to think of interviewing as a process that turns others into subjects so that their words can be appropriated for the benefit of the researcher. Daphne Patai (1987) raises a similar issue when she points out that the Brazilian women she interviewed seemed to enjoy the activity, but she was deeply troubled by the possibility that she was exploiting them for her scholarship.

Interviewing as exploitation is a serious concern and provides a contradiction and a tension within my work that I have not fully resolved. Part of the issue is, as Patai recognizes, an economic one. Steps can be taken to assure that participants receive an equitable share of whatever financial profits ensue from their participation in research. But, at a deeper level, there is a more basic question of research for whom, by whom, and to what end. Research is often done by people in relative positions of power in the guise of reform. All too often the only interests served are those of the researcher's personal advancement. It is a constant struggle to make the research process equitable, especially in the United States where a good deal of our social structure is inequitable.

CONCLUSION

So why choose interviewing? Perhaps constitutive events in your life, as in mine, have added up to your being "interested" in interviewing as a method. It is a powerful way to gain insight into educational and other important social issues through understanding the experience of the individuals whose lives reflect those issues. As a method of inquiry, interviewing is most consistent with people's ability to make meaning through language. It affirms the importance of the individual without denigrating the possibility of community and collaboration. Finally, it is deeply satisfying to researchers who are interested in others' stories.

NOTE

1. The word a researcher chooses to refer to the person being interviewed often communicates important information about the researcher's purpose in interviewing and his or her view of the relationship. In the literature about interviewing, a wide range of terms is used. *Interviewee* or *respondent* (Lincoln & Guba, 1985; Richardson, Dohrenwend, & Klein, 1965) casts the participant in a passive role and the process of interviewing as one of giving answers to questions. Some writers refer to the person being interviewed as the *subject* (Patai, 1987). On one hand, this term can be seen as positive; it changes the person being interviewed from object to subject. On the other hand, the term *subject* implies that the interviewing relationship is hierarchical and that the person being interviewed can be subjugated. Alternatively, anthropologists tend to use the term *informant* (Ellen, 1984), because the people they interview inform them about a culture. Researchers pursuing cooperative inquiry and action research may consider all involved in the research as *co-researchers* (Reason, 1994). The use of this term has significant implications for how you design research, and gather and interpret data.

In searching for the term we wanted to use, my colleagues and I focused on the fact that in-depth interviewing encourages people to reconstruct their experience actively within the context of their lives. To reflect that active stance we chose the word *participants* to refer to the people we interview. That word seems to capture both the sense of active involvement that occurs in an in-depth interview and the sense of equity that we try to build in our interviewing relationships.

Chapter 2

A Structure for In-Depth, Phenomenological Interviewing

T he word *interviewing* covers a wide range of practices. There are tightly structured, survey interviews with preset, standardized, normally closed questions. At the other end of the continuum are open-ended, apparently unstructured, anthropological interviews that might be seen almost, according to Spradley (1979), as friendly conversations. (For a description of the wide range of approaches to interviewing, see Bertaux, 1981; Briggs, 1986, p. 20; Ellen, 1984, p. 231; Kvale, 1996; Lincoln & Guba, 1985, pp. 268–269; Mishler, 1986, pp. 14–15; Richardson, Dohrenwend, & Klein, 1965, pp. 36–40; Rubin & Rubin, 1995; Spradley, 1979, pp. 57–58.)

This book, however, is about what I and my colleagues have come to call in-depth, phenomenologically based interviewing. The method combines life-history interviewing (see Bertaux, 1981) and focused, in-depth interviewing informed by assumptions drawn from phenomenology and especially from Alfred Schutz (1967). The structure of the interviews I describe in this chapter and the approach to interviewing technique and data analysis I describe in later chapters follow from these theoretical positions. (For an extended discussion of the relationship between the techniques of interviewing and the theoretical underpinning of one's approach to interviewing, see Kvale, 1996, chap 3.)

In this approach interviewers use, primarily, open-ended questions. Their major task is to build upon and explore their participants' responses to those questions. The goal is to have the participant reconstruct his or her experience within the topic under study.

The range of topics adaptable to this interviewing approach is wide, covering almost any issue involving the experience of contemporary people. In past years, doctoral students with whom I have worked or had contact have explored the following subjects for their dissertations and further publications:

Eleventh-grade students as writers (Cleary, 1985, 1988, 1991)
Student teaching in urban schools (Compagnone, 1995)
English teachers' experiences in their first year of teaching
    (Cook, 2004)
Relationship between theoretical orientation to reading
    and reading practices (Elliot-Johns, 2004; received the
    Canadian Association for Teacher Education's Outstanding
    Dissertation Award in 2005.)
The experience of mainland Chinese women in American
    graduate programs (Frank, 2000)
Black jazz musicians who become teachers in colleges and
    universities (Hardin, 1987)
The experience of students whose first language is not English
    in mainstream English classrooms (Gabriel, 1997)
African-American performing artists who teach at traditionally
    white colleges (Jenoure, 1995)
Advising in a land grant university (Lynch, 1997)
Gender issues embedded in student teaching (Miller, 1993, 1997)
The literacy experience of vocational high school students
    (Nagle, 1995, 2001)
The impact of tracking on student teachers (O'Donnell, 1990)
Women returning to community colleges (Schatzkamer, 1986)
The work of physical education teacher educators (Williamson,
    1988, 1990)
Lesbian physical education teachers (Woods, 1990)
The experience of young Black fathers in a fatherhood program
    (Whiting, 2004)
ESL teachers (Young, 1990)

In each of these pilot and dissertation studies, the interviewer explored complex issues in the subject area by examining the concrete experience of people in that area and the meaning their experience had for them.

THE THREE-INTERVIEW SERIES

Perhaps most distinguishing of all its features, this model of in-depth, phenomenological interviewing involves conducting a series of three separate interviews with each participant. People's behavior becomes meaningful and understandable when placed in the context of their lives and the lives of those around them. Without context there is little possibility of exploring the meaning of an experience (Patton, 1989). Interviewers who propose to explore their topic by arranging a one-shot meeting with an "interviewee" whom they have never met tread on thin contextual ice. (See Locke, Silverman, & Spirduso, 2004, pp. 209–226, for important insights on this issue in particular and qualitative research in general from the perspective of the readers of such research. Also see Mishler, 1986.)

Dolbeare and Schuman (Schuman, 1982) designed the series of three interviews that characterizes this approach and allows the interviewer and participant to plumb the experience and to place it in context. The first interview establishes the context of the participants' experience. The second allows participants to reconstruct the details of their experience within the context in which it occurs. And the third encourages the participants to reflect on the meaning their experience holds for them.

Interview One: Focused Life History

In the first interview, the interviewer's task is to put the participant's experience in context by asking him or her to tell as much as possible about him or herself in light of the topic up to the present time. In our study of the experience of student teachers and mentors in a professional development school in East Longmeadow, Massachusetts (O'Donnell et al., 1989), we asked our participants to tell us about their past lives, up until the time they became student teachers or mentors, going as far back as possible within 90 minutes.

We ask them to reconstruct their early experiences in their families, in school, with friends, in their neighborhood, and at work. Because the topic of this interview study is their experience as student teachers or as mentors, we focus on the participants' past experience in school and in any situations such as camp counseling, tutoring, or coaching they might have done before coming to the professional development school program.

In asking them to put their student teaching or mentoring in the context of their life history, we avoid asking, "Why did you become a student teacher (or mentor)?" Instead, we ask how they came to be participating in the program. By asking "how?" we hope to have them reconstruct and narrate a range of constitutive events in their past family, school, and work experience that place their participation in the professional development school program in the context of their lives. (See Gergen, 2001, for an introduction to the power of narratives for self-definition.)

Interview Two: The Details of Experience

The purpose of the second interview is to concentrate on the con-crete details of the participants' present lived experience in the topic area of the study. We ask them to reconstruct these details. In our study of student teachers and mentors in a clinical site, for example, we ask them what they actually do on the job. We do not ask for opinions but rather the details of their experience, upon which their opinions may be built. According to Freeman Dyson (2004), a famous mathematician named Littlewood, who was Dyson's teacher at the University of Cambridge, estimated that during the time we are awake and actually engaged in our lives, we see and hear things at about a rate of one per second. So in an 8-hour day, we are involved in perhaps 30,000 events. In this second interview, then, our task is to strive, however incompletely, to reconstruct the myriad details of our participants' experiences in the area we are studying.

In order to put their experience within the context of the social set-ting, we ask the student teachers, for example, to talk about their relation-ships with their students, their mentors, the other faculty in the school, the administrators, the parents, and the wider community. In this second interview, we might ask them to reconstruct a day in their student teach-ing from the moment they woke up to the time they fell asleep. We ask for stories about their experience in school as a way of eliciting details.

Interview Three: Reflection on the Meaning

In the third interview, we ask participants to reflect on the meaning of their experience. The question of "meaning" is not one of satisfac-tion or reward, although such issues may play a part in the participants' thinking. Rather, it addresses the intellectual and emotional connections between the participants' work and life. The question might be phrased, "Given what you have said about your life before you became a mentor teacher and given what you have said about your work now, how do you understand mentoring in your life? What sense does it make to you?" This question may take a future orientation; for example, "Given what you have reconstructed in these interviews, where do you see yourself going in the future?"

Making sense or making meaning requires that the participants look at how the factors in their lives interacted to bring them to their pres-ent situation. It also requires that they look at their present experience in detail and within the context in which it occurs. The combination of exploring the past to clarify the events that led participants to where they are now, and describing the concrete details of their present experience, establishes conditions for reflecting upon what they are now doing in their lives. The third interview can be productive only if the foundation for it has been established in the first two.

Even though it is in the third interview that we focus on the participants' understanding of their experience, through all three interviews participants are making meaning. The very process of putting experience into language is a meaning-making process (Vygotsky, 1987). When we ask participants to reconstruct details of their experience, they are selecting events from their past and in so doing imparting meaning to them. When we ask participants to tell stories of their experience, they frame some aspect of it with a beginning, a middle, and an end and thereby make it meaningful, whether it is in interview one, two, or three. But in interview three, we focus on that question in the context of the two previous interviews and make that meaning making the center of our attention.

RESPECT THE STRUCTURE

We have found it important to adhere to the three-interview structure. Each interview serves a purpose both by itself and within the series. Sometimes, in the first interview, a participant may start to tell an interesting story about his or her present work situation; but that is the focus of the second interview. It is tempting, because the information may be interesting, to pursue the participant's lead and forsake the structure of the interview. To do so, however, can erode the focus of each interview and the interviewer's sense of purpose. Each interview comprises a multitude of decisions that the interviewer must make. The open-ended, in-depth inquiry is best carried out in a structure that allows both the participant and the interviewer to maintain a sense of the focus of each interview in the series.

Furthermore, each interview provides a foundation of detail that helps illumine the next. Taking advantage of the interactive and cumulative nature of the sequence of the interviews requires that interviewers adhere to the purpose of each. There is a logic to the interviews, and to lose control of their direction is to lose the power of that logic and the benefit from it. Therefore, in the process of conducting the three interviews, the interviewer must maintain a delicate balance between providing enough openness for the participants to tell their stories and enough focus to allow the interview structure to work. (See McCracken, 1988, p. 22, for further discussion of this delicate balance.)

LENGTH OF INTERVIEWS

To accomplish the purpose of each of the three interviews, Dolbeare and Schuman (Schuman, 1982) used a 90-minute format. People learning this method for the first time often react, "Oh, that is so long. How will we fill that amount of time? How will we get a participant to agree to be interviewed for that length of time?"

An hour carries with it the consciousness of a standard unit of time that can have participants "watching the clock." Two hours seems too long to sit at one time. Given that the purpose of this approach is to have the participants reconstruct their experience, put it in the context of their lives, and reflect on its meaning, anything shorter than 90 minutes for each interview seems too short. There is, however, nothing magical or absolute about this time frame. For younger participants, a shorter period may be appropriate. What is important is that the length of time be decided upon before the interview process begins.

Doing so gives unity to each interview; the interview has at least a chronological beginning, middle, and end. Interviewers can learn to hone their skills if they work within a set amount of time and have to fit their technique to it. Furthermore, if interviewers are dealing with a considerable number of participants, they need to schedule their interviews so that they can finish one and go on to the next. As they begin to work with the vast amount of material that is generated in in-depth interviews, they will appreciate having allotted a limited amount of time to each.

The participants have a stake in a set amount of time also. They must know how much time is being asked of them; they have to schedule their lives. Moreover, an open-ended time period can produce undue anxiety. Most participants with whom I have worked come very quickly to appreciate the 90-minute period. Rather than seeming too long, it's long enough to make them feel they are being taken seriously.

At times it is tempting to keep going at the end of the 90 minutes, because what is being discussed at that point is of considerable interest. Although one might gain new insights by continuing the interview beyond the allotted time, it is my experience that a situation of diminishing returns sets in. Extending the interview causes an unraveling of the interviewer's purpose and of the participant's confidence that the interviewer will do what he or she promised.

A related phenomenon is that sometimes participants continue to talk after the interview is concluded and the tape is turned off. It is tempting to continue, because the participants seem suddenly willing to discuss matters heretofore avoided. The problem is that such after-the-fact conversations are not recorded and are not normally covered in the written consent form. (See Chapter 5.) Although the material may seem interesting, it is ultimately difficult to use.

SPACING OF INTERVIEWS

The three-interview structure works best, in my experience, when the researcher can space each interview from 3 days to a week apart. This allows time for the participant to mull over the preceding interview but not enough time to lose the connection between the two. In addition, the spacing allows interviewers to work with the participants over a 2- to 3-week period. This passage of time reduces the impact of possibly idiosyncratic interviews. That is, the participant might be having a terrible day, be sick, or be distracted in such a way as to affect the quality of a particular interview.

In addition, the fact that interviewers come back to talk three times for an 1½ hours affects the development of the relationship between the participants and the interviewers positively. The interviewers are asking a lot of the participants; but the interviewers reciprocate with their time and effort. With the contact visits, the telephone calls and letters to confirm schedules and appointments (see Chapter 4), and the three actual interviews, interviewers have an opportunity to establish a substantial relationship with participants over time.

ALTERNATIVES TO THE STRUCTURE AND PROCESS

Researchers will have reasons for exploring alternatives to the structure and procedures described above. As long as a structure is maintained that allows participants to reconstruct and reflect upon their experience within the context of their lives, alterations to the three-interview structure and the duration and spacing of interviews can certainly be explored. But too extreme a bending of the form may result in your not being able to take advantage of the intent of the structure.

Our research teams have tried variations in spacing, usually necessitated by the schedules of our participants. On occasion, when a participant missed an interview because of an unanticipated complication, we conducted interviews one and two during the same afternoon rather than spacing them a few days or a week apart. And sometimes participants have been unavailable for 2 or 3 weeks. Once a participant said he was leaving for summer vacation the day after we contacted him. We conducted interviews one, two, and three with him all on the same day with reasonable results.

As yet there are no absolutes in the world of interviewing. Relatively little research has been done on the effects of following one procedure over others; most extant research has conceived of interviewing in a stimulus-response frame of reference, which is inadequate to the in-depth procedure (Brenner, Brown, & Canter, 1985; Hyman, Cobb, Fledman, Hart, & Stember, 1954; Kahn & Cannell, 1960; Mishler, 1986; Richardson et al., 1965). The governing principle in designing interviewing projects might well be to strive for a rational process that is both repeatable and documentable. Remember that it is not a perfect world. It is almost always better to conduct an interview under less than ideal conditions than not to conduct one at all.

WHOSE MEANING IS IT? VALIDITY AND RELIABILITY

Whose meaning is it that an interview brings forth and that a researcher reports in a presentation, article, or book? That is not a simple question. Every aspect of the structure, process, and practice of interviewing can be directed toward the goal of minimizing the effect the interviewer and the interviewing situation have on how the participants reconstruct their experience. No matter how diligently we work to that effect, however, the fact is that interviewers are a part of the interviewing picture. They ask questions, respond to the participant, and at times even share their own experiences. Moreover, interviewers work with the material, select from it, interpret, describe, and analyze it. Though they may be disciplined and dedicated to keeping the interviews as the participants' meaning-making process, interviewers are also a part of that process (Ferrarotti, 1981; Kvale, 1996; Mishler, 1986).

The interaction between the data gatherers and the participants is inherent in the nature of interviewing. It is inherent, as well, in other qualitative approaches, such as participant observation. And I believe it is also inherent in most experimental and quasi-experimental methodologies applied to human beings, despite the myriad and sophisticated measures developed to control for it (Campbell & Stanley, 1963).

One major difference, however, between qualitative and quantitative approaches is that in in-depth interviewing we recognize and affirm the role of the instrument, the human interviewer. Rather than decrying the fact that the instrument used to gather data affects this process, we say the human interviewer can be a marvelously smart, adaptable, flexible instrument who can respond to situations with skill, tact, and understanding (Lincoln & Guba, 1985, p. 107).

Although the interviewer can strive to have the meaning being made in the interview as much a function of the participant's reconstruction and reflection as possible, the interviewer must nevertheless recognize that the meaning is, to some degree, a function of the participant's interaction with the interviewer. Only by recognizing that interaction and affirming its possibilities can interviewers use their skills (see Chapter 6) to minimize the distortion (see Patton, 1989, p. 157) that can occur because of their role in the interview.

Is It Anybody's Meaning?

How do we know that what the participant is telling us is true? And if it is true for this participant, is it true for anyone else? And if another person were doing the interview, would we get a different meaning? Or if we were to do the interview at a different time of year, would the participant reconstruct his or her experience differently? Or if we had picked different participants to interview, would we get an entirely dissimilar and perhaps contradictory sense of the issue at hand? These are some of the questions underlying the issues of validity, reliability, and generalizability that researchers confront.

Many qualitative researchers disagree with the epistemological assumptions underlying the notion of validity. They argue for a new vocabulary and rhetoric with which to discuss validity and reliability (Mishler, 1986, pp. 108–110). Lincoln and Guba (1985), for example, substitute the notion of "trustworthiness" for that of validity. In a careful exposition they argue that qualitative researchers must inform what they do by concepts of "credibility," "transferability," "dependability," and "confirmability" (pp. 289–332).

Others criticize the idea of objectivity that underlies notions of reliability and validity. Kvale (1996) sees the issue of validity as a question of the "quality of craftsmanship" of the researchers as they make defensible knowledge claims (pp. 241–244). Ferrarotti (1981) argues that the most profound knowledge can be gained only by the deepest intersubjectivity among researchers and that which they are researching. Such a discussion suggests that neither the vocabulary of "validity" nor "trustworthiness" is adequate.

Yet, in-depth interviewers can respond to the question, "Are the participant's comments valid?" The three-interview structure incorporates features that enhance the accomplishment of validity. It places participants' comments in context. It encourages interviewing participants over the course of 1 to 3 weeks to account for idiosyncratic days and to check for the internal consistency of what they say. Furthermore, by interviewing a number of participants, we can connect their experiences and check the comments of one participant against those of others. Finally, the goal of the process is to understand how our participants understand and make meaning of their experience. If the interview structure works to allow them to make sense to themselves as well as to the interviewer, then it has gone a long way toward validity.

An Example of an Approach to Validity

One participant in our Secondary Teacher Education Program was a woman who had taught in parochial schools for a number of years but was not certified. She had enrolled in our program to get certified at the high school level in social studies. She agreed to be interviewed about her experience in our clinical site teacher education program.

The interviewer began her third interview with its basic question: "What does it mean to you to be a student teacher?" She responded:

> Well, I guess–well, . . . [small laugh]–it kinda–it really kind
> of means that I've finally gotten down to actually trying to–I
> guess what it means is–[it] is the final passage into making
> a commitment to this, the profession, to teaching as–as a
> profession. What am I going to do with my life because I have
> all–all this time, going up and down and in and out of teaching.
> Should I or shouldn't I? I was kind of stuck in that space where
> people say, you know, "Oh, those who can't, teach. Those
> who can, do." Just the whole negative status that teaching and
> education have. So it's kind of fraught with that. And really
> resisting the fact that I had to student teach. I mean, I can

remember [that] holding me back, what, 10 years ago, thinking, "Oh, no, I will actually have to be a student teacher some day," and remembered what student teachers were like in my high school, and thinking, "Oh, I'll never humiliate myself that way." [small laugh] And so I guess it was the final–[pause]–biting the bullet to . . . making a commitment.

Is what she says valid? In the first interview she recounted how she had dropped out of college and taught in elementary grades in parochial schools because she needed money. In that interview she also talked about how she had dropped out of education courses because she didn't think she was getting enough out of them; how she had switched to an academic field, but later realized that she really liked teaching.

The material in her third interview is internally consistent with the material in her first, which was given 2 weeks earlier. Internal consistency over a period of time leads one to trust that she is not lying to the interviewer. Furthermore, there is enough in the syntax, the pauses, the groping for words, the self-effacing laughter, to make a reader believe that she is grappling seriously with the question of what student teaching means to her, and that what she is saying is true for her at the time she is saying it.

Moreover, in reading the transcript, we see that the interviewer has kept quiet, not interrupted her, not tried to redirect her thinking while she was developing it; so her thoughts seem to be hers and not the interviewer's. These are her words, and they reflect her understanding of her experience at the time of her interview.

When I read this passage, I learned something both about this particular student and about an aspect of the student-teaching experience that had not really been apparent to me. I began to think about aspects of the process we require prior to student teaching that enhance the need for students to make a commitment and about other aspects of our program that minimize that need. I began to wonder what the conditions are that encourage a person to make that commitment.

Finally, what the participant said about the status of education as a career and how that related to her personal indecision is consistent with what we know the literature says about the teaching profession and with what other participants in our study have said. I can relate this individual passage to a broader discourse on the issue.

The interview allowed me to get closer to understanding this student teacher's experience than I would have been able to do by other methods such as questionnaires or observation. I cannot say that her understanding of student teaching as a commitment is valid for others, although passages in other interviews connect to what she has said. I can say that it seems valid for her at this point in her life. I cannot say that her understanding of the meaningfulness of student teaching as a commitment she had heretofore not been willing to make will not change. Unlike the laws of physics, the rules governing human life and social interaction are always changing—except that we die. There is no solid, unmovable platform upon which to base our understanding of human affairs. They are in constant flux. Heisenberg's principle of indeterminacy (Lincoln & Guba, 1985; Polanyi, 1958) speaks at least as directly to human affairs as it does to the world of physics.

The structure of the three interviews, the passage of time over which the interviews occur, the internal consistency and possible external consistency of the passages, the syntax, diction, and even nonverbal aspects of the passage, and the discovery and sense of learning that I get from reading the passage lead me to have confidence in its authenticity. Because we are concerned with the participant's understanding of her experience, the authenticity of what she is saying makes it reasonable for me to have confidence in its validity for her.

Avoiding a Mechanistic Response

There is room in the universe for multiple approaches to validity. The problem is not in the multiplicity. Rather it lies in the sometimes doctrinaire ways some advocates of divergent approaches polarize the issue. (See Gage, 1989.) Those who advocate qualitative approaches are in danger of becoming as doctrinaire as those who once held the monopoly on educational research and advocated quantitative approaches.

On occasion I see dissertations in which doctoral candidates are as mechanical about establishing an "audit trail" or devising methods of "triangularization" (Lincoln & Guba, 1985, p. 283) as those in my generation who dutifully devised procedures to confront "instrument decay" and "experimental mortality" (Campbell & Stanley, 1963, pp. 79, 182). What are needed are not formulaic approaches to enhancing either validity or trustworthiness but understanding of and respect for the issues that underlie those terms. We must grapple with them, doing our best to increase our ways of knowing and of avoiding ignorance, realizing that our efforts are quite small in the larger scale of things. (For a "common sense" approach to validity, see Maxwell, 1996. For a "craftsmanship" approach to validity, see Kvale, 1996. For a highly personal view of validity, see Wolcott, 1994.)

EXPERIENCE THE PROCESS YOURSELF

Before readers go much further with this approach to interviewing, I recommend that they test their interest in it and explore some of the issues by doing a practice project. Team up with a peer. Interview each other about your experience in your present job or as a graduate student. (If you are doing this practice project as part of a class, this exercise can lead to some significant understanding about what graduate study is like in your school.)

Use the three-interview structure. Because this is practice to become acquainted with the technique, shorten, if you choose to do so, the time normally allotted to each interview from 90 minutes to 30 minutes. In the first interview, ask your peer participant about how she came to her work or her graduate study. Find out as much as possible about the context of her life leading up to her present position or to her status as a graduate student.

In the second interview, ask your participant to tell you as much as possible about the details of her job experience or her work as a graduate student. Ask, "What is your work? What is it like for you to do what you do?"

In the third interview, ask your participant what her work or her experience as a graduate student means to her. You might say, "Now that you have talked about how you came to your work (or to be a graduate student), and what it is like for you to do that work (or be a student), what does it mean to you?"

Arrange appointments for each of the interviews. Tape-record them, and be sure to arrange to be interviewed by your peer participant in return.

The point of this practice project is to experience interviewing and being interviewed and to see whether you connect to the possibilities of the process. The practice project should alert you to how the way you are as a person affects your interviewing. You may notice how difficult it is for you to stay quiet and let another person speak while at the same time being an active listener and following up on what your participant has said. You may become aware of issues of control and focus. You may find that you have little patience for or interest in other people's stories; or you may connect to their possibilities.

Chapter 3

Proposing Research:
From Mind to Paper to Action

Research-proposal writing is substantively and symbolically an important event. In an excellent book on the subject, *Proposals That Work*, Locke, Spirduso, and Silverman (2000) say that a dissertation proposal has three substantive functions: to plan, to communicate, and to establish a contract. There is, however, a fourth function. Developing a dissertation proposal and getting it approved is a crucial step in the rite of passage of earning a doctorate. Its ritualistic function can sometimes make writing a proposal seem daunting. It transforms the writer of the proposal from the status of student to that of researcher.

RESEARCH PROPOSALS AS RITES OF PASSAGE

In some respects becoming an academic is like joining a club. As in most other somewhat-exclusive clubs, there are those who are in and those who are out; there are elites and non-elites. There are privileges of membership, and there are penalties for not paying dues. To some extent, success in the club is a matter of merit; but that success is sometimes affected by issues of race, gender, and class that can influence entry into the club in the first place, or weight the power of those who have been admitted already.

Although pressures, strains, and contradictions affect those who work in collegiate institutions just as they do those who work in others, still, college faculty are paid for the pleasurable activities of reading, writing, teaching, and doing research. Relative to public school teachers, for example, we have a great deal of autonomy over our time and professional lives. Not all doctoral candidates in education move on to faculty positions in colleges or universities. But those who use their doctorates to assume leadership positions in school systems often gain a degree of autonomy in their working lives that many would envy.

Those who have already earned the doctorate often act as gatekeepers to the club. During the rituals of proposal submission, review, and approval established by the gatekeepers, the power relationship between candidate and doctoral advisor is very unequal. (See Locke et al., 2000, chap. 2, for further discussion of dysfunctions that can occur between doctoral candidates and faculty mentors.) Elements of sexism, racism, classism, and institutional politics can enter the process. When that relationship is inequitable, the rite of passage can be excessively anxiety producing. It takes a great deal of thoughtfulness on everyone's part to make the relationship between doctoral candidate and committee equitable at the proposal stage.

COMMITMENT

When a candidate's doctoral program is working well, a research topic arises out of work that has gone before. Course work, fieldwork, practica, clinical work, and comprehensive exams all lead the candidate forward to an area of inquiry about which he or she feels some passion. If the doctoral program has not worked well—if committee memberships have changed, if the doctoral student has been convinced against his or her own interests to pursue those of a professor—a student can progress through the earlier stages of the rite of passage without identifying a topic that is personally meaningful. Kenneth Liberman (1999, p. 51) notes that if doctoral candidates do not really believe in their topic and are not motivated by the intrinsic values of their own research topics, their work can lack a sense of authenticity. In such a situation, the writing of a proposal may be more excruciating than satisfying.

In some cases doctoral candidates enter the program having already chosen a topic. For a while they make their peers nervous because they seem so advanced and confident. My sense is that such confidence is often misplaced. The experience of the doctoral program itself should bring about some sort of new orientation, some interest in new areas, some growth in the candidate's outlook. If it does not, the candidate is looking backward instead of forward.

Substantively, one of the underlying reasons for writing a proposal is its planning function (Locke et al., 2000). Although Joseph Maxwell in his thoughtful book, *Qualitative Research Design* (1996), separates the process of research design from proposal writing, my experience is that the writing of the proposal is a prime opportunity for doctoral candidates to clarify their research design. To plan, candidates must assess where they have been and make a commitment to where they would like to go. This can be a stressful part of the process.

I remember one outstanding doctoral candidate who was stalled for 6 months at the prospect of writing his dissertation proposal. It was not that he could not find a subject; nor was he in search of a method. He was just frozen in his writing. After 6 months of not being able to get around his writing block, he finally discussed his anxieties about, in effect, changing club memberships. He said that he had grown up in a working-class neighborhood where people sat on their front-porch steps in the summer drinking beer. That was what his parents still did. He was not sure that he wanted to leave the front porch to start drinking white wine in the living room at faculty gatherings. For many doctoral candidates, completing their dissertations implies a commitment to a new professional and personal identity that can be difficult to make. In many ways writing a dissertation proposal is a key step in the developmental process that occurs in doctoral study, and such processes are seldom free of significant complexities.

FROM THOUGHT TO LANGUAGE

Many students have trouble writing proposals because they are plagued by a sense of audience. The process seems dominated by doctoral committees and Institutional Review Boards that must approve the proposed research. (For more on Institutional Review Boards, see Chapter 5.) When audience plays such a dominating role, writing can easily suffer. Rather than concentrating on what he or she wants to say, the candidate may filter every sentence through the screen of what is expected and what will be acceptable to the committee.

Preliminary ideas about research often stay locked in one's inner speech. They are fleeting, predicated, and unstable (Vygotsky, 1987), making communication of them difficult. However, those ideas in inner speech must be made explicit. Doctoral candidates do have to communicate clearly to their committee what they are thinking.

A key to communicating about plans for research is to focus first on what is meaningful. When a proposal works best, it emanates from the motives of the candidate and works its way through thought, inner speech, and into external speech through meaning. Often, however, the form and substance of the inquiry in a dissertation proposal can seem to the candidate to be imposed from the outside; the format of dissertation proposals can seem to take precedence over their substance. Then the writing of the proposal can become mechanical and formulaic.

WHAT IS TO BE DONE?

Peter Elbow (1981) offers an approach to writing that I think can be useful in such cases. He suggests that trying both to create with the audience in mind and to make writing perfect from the start imposes an undue burden on the writing process. He suggests making writing and editing two separate aspects of the writing process. And he urges deferring thoughts of the audience until the editing part of the process.

To facilitate that separation, Elbow suggests what has come to be known as free-writing and focused free-writing. Focused free-writing is a process that allows the writer to concentrate on the topic and forget the audience. It advises writers to start writing on their topics and to continue for a specified period of time without stopping. If they get stuck, they should repeat their last word or write the word *stuck* until they get going again. A person new to the process might begin with 5 minutes of focused free-writing, gradually increasing the length of time.

After free-writing sections of the proposal, writers can then select from these the most cogent, refashioning from them a first draft. Elbow suggests other methods to help writers overcome blocks due to anxiety about audience. Near the end of the writing process, rather than at the beginning, writers can edit their drafts with the audience and the form of dissertation proposal in mind. I recommend Elbow's *Writing With Power* (1981); Locke, Spirduso, and Silverman's *Proposals That Work* (2000); Maxwell's *Qualitative Research Design* (1996); and Schram's *Conceptualizing Qualitative Inquiry* (2003) as important resources for anyone about to write a dissertation proposal.

QUESTIONS TO STRUCTURE THE PROPOSAL

What?

Proposal writers need to ask themselves some simple questions. These can be divided into several groups. First is a group of questions I put under the heading of "What?" In what am I interested? What am I trying to learn about and understand? What is the basis of my interest?

Interviewers begin with an interest in a particular area. At the beginning of interviewers' research lurks the desire to understand what is going on. But how did that desire begin? Important questions that must be asked in interviewing research and that are seldom asked in experimental or quasi-experimental research are, What is the context of my interest? How did I come to this interest? What is my stake in the inquiry, and what do I get out of pursuing my interest and learning about it? What are my expectations about the subject of inquiry?

Research, like almost everything else in life, has autobiographical roots. It is crucial for interviewers to identify the autobiographical roots of their interest in their topic. (See Locke, Silverman & Spirduso, 2004, pp. 217–218, for a compelling discussion of this issue.) Research is hard work; interviewing research is especially so. In order to sustain the energy needed to do the research well, a researcher must have some passion about his or her subject. Rather than seeking a "disinterested" position as a researcher, the interviewer needs to understand and affirm his or her interest in order to build on the energy that can come from it. Equally important, researchers must identify the source of their interest in order to channel it appropriately. They must acknowledge it in order to minimize the distortion such interest can cause in the way they carry out their interviewing. An autobiographical section explaining researchers' connections to their proposed research seems to me to be crucial for those interested in in-depth interviewing. (For an example of such an explanation, see Maxwell, 1996, pp. 123–124.)

Finally, interviewers must not only identify their connection with the subject of the interview; they must also affirm that their interest in the subject reflects a real desire to know what is going on, to understand the experience. If, in fact, interviewers are so intimately connected to the subject of inquiry that they really do not feel perplexed, and what they are really hoping to do is corroborate their own experience, they will not have enough distance from the subject to interview effectively. The questions will not be real; that is, they will not be questions to which the interviewers do not already have the answers.

There is, therefore, an inherent paradox at the heart of the issue of what topics researchers choose to study. On the one hand, they must choose topics that engage their interest, their passion, and sustain their motivation for the labor-intensive work that interviewing research is. That usually means in some way or another they must be close to their topics. On the other hand, to be open to the process of listening and careful exploration that is crucial in an interviewing study, they must approach their research interests with a certain sense of naiveté, innocence, and absence of prejudgments (Moustakas, 1994, p. 85). Researchers who can negotiate that complex tension will be able to listen intently, ask real questions, and set the stage for working well with the material they gather.

Why? in Context

The next question to ask is why the subject might be important to others. Why is the subject significant? What is the background of this subject, and why is that background important to understand? To what else does the subject relate? If you understand the complexities of this subject, what will be the benefit and who will obtain it? What is the context of previous work that has been done on the subject (Locke et al., 2000)? How will your work build on what has been done already? (See Locke et al., 2000; Rubin & Rubin, 1995, for succinct discussions of the issue of significance.)

Locke and his colleagues are especially cogent in their discussion of what often appears in dissertation proposals as "reviews of the literature." They stress that these sometimes mechanical summaries of previous research miss the intent of reading the literature connected to the subject. Such reading should inform researchers of the context of the research, allow them to gain a better sense of the issue's significance and how it has been approached before, as well as reveal what is missing in the previous research. These understandings can be integrated into the various sections of the proposal and do not necessitate a separate one that sometimes reads like a book report. (See Locke et al., 2000, pp. 63–68, and Maxwell, 1996, chap. 3, who is also thoughtful on this issue.)

In addition to asking why the topic is historically significant, critical ethnographers suggest that how the topic relates to issues of power, justice, and oppression must also be raised. Especially important are the issues of power that are implicit in the research topic itself (Solsken, 1989) and in interviewing as a methodology. John Rowan (1981) suggests that researchers consider not only how their own personal interests are served by their research but also who else's interest is served. What about the participants in the research? What do they get out of participating? What do they risk? Does the research underwrite any existing patterns of oppression? Or does the research offer some possibility of understanding that could create liberating energy? In a world beset by inequity, why is the topic of research important? (See Fay, 1987, for an important discussion of the foundations of critical social science.)

How?

A next question to ask is, How? Assuming that researchers have decided that in-depth interviewing is appropriate for their study, how can they adapt the structure of in-depth, phenomenological interviewing outlined in Chapter 2 to their subject of study? I offer examples of such adaptations by two doctoral students who have worked with this approach to interviewing. (I share results of their work in the Appendix.)

Marguerite Sheehan (1989), who was a doctoral candidate in early childhood education at the University of Massachusetts, addressed the question as follows. She was interested in studying child care as a career. In her review of the literature she had found that most of the research on child-care providers focused on those who had left the field early because of what was called "burn-out." Sheehan was interested in people who stayed in the field, especially those who saw providing child care as a career. She hoped to come to understand the nature of their experience and to see if she could unravel some of the factors that contributed to their longevity in the field. Sheehan took the three-interview structure and adapted it as follows:

> *Interview One* (life history): How did the participant come to be a
>   child-care provider? A review of the participant's life history
>   up to the time he or she became a child-care provider.
> *Interview Two* (contemporary experience): What is it like for the
>   participant to be a child-care provider? What are the details
>   of the participant's work as a child-care provider?
> *Interview Three* (reflection on meaning): What does it mean to
>   the participant to be a child-care provider? Given what the
>   participant has said in interviews one and two, how does he
>   or she make sense of his or her work as a child-care provider?

Toon Fuderich (1995), who also was a doctoral candidate at the School of Education of the University of Massachusetts, was interested in studying the experience of Cambodian refugees who as children had experienced the terrors of war. She adapted her interest in this topic to the three-interview structure as follows:

> *Interview One* (life history): How did the participant become
>   a refugee? What was the participant's life history before
>   coming to the United States?

Interview Two (contemporary experience): What is life like for
the participant in the United States? What is her education,
work, and family life like?

Interview Three (reflection on meaning): What does it mean to
the participant to be living in the United States now? How
does she make sense of her present life in the context of her
life experience?

Who? When? Where?

The next set of questions asks whom the researchers will interview,
and how they will get access and make contact with their participants.
In Chapter 4 we discuss the complexities of access, contact, and selecting participants. What is called for at this point is a consideration of the
strategy the researchers will use. What will the range of participants be?
What strategy of gaining access to them will the researchers use? How
will they make contact with the participants? The strategy may allow
for a process of participant selection that evolves over the course of the
study, but the structure and strategy for that selection must be thought
out in the proposal.

Some writers suggest that the "how" of a qualitative research study
can itself be emergent as the study proceeds. That orientation assumes
that because qualitative research does not begin with a set of hypotheses to test, strict control of variables is not necessary. Furthermore,
because the inquiry is being done in order to learn about complexities
of which researchers are not totally aware, the design and even the
focus of the study have to be seen as "emergent" (Lincoln & Guba,
1985, pp. 208–211, pp. 224–225) or "flexible" (Rubin & Rubin, 1995,
pp. 43–48).

Although it is understandable that researchers would want to build
flexibility into a research design, there is a danger in overemphasizing the
"emergent" nature of research design in qualitative research. To the inexperienced, it can appear to minimize the need for careful preparation and
planning. It can lead to the notion that qualitative research is somehow an
"art" that really is incommunicable, or that somehow those who engage
in it have earned a special status because they do not share the assumptions of those who do what is called quantitative research (McCracken,
1988, pp. 12–13). The danger of overemphasizing the "emergent" nature
of the design of the study is a looseness, lack of focus, and misplaced non-
chalance about purpose, method, and procedure on the part of those who

do qualitative research. Lincoln and Guba (1985) themselves stress that the emergent nature of qualitative research cannot be used as a license for "undisciplined and haphazard 'poking around'" (p. 251).

RATIONALE

Although the paradigms that underlie research methods in the social sciences seem to be changing rapidly (Kvale, 1996; Lincoln & Guba, 1985), the extent to which researchers will have to defend their use of in-depth interviewing as their research methodology will depend on their individual departments. Some are still dominated by experimentalism or other forms of quantitative research. In others there may be a predisposition to experimental and quasi-experimental methods but nevertheless openness to qualitative research. In still others there may be a strong preference for qualitative research among a significant number of the faculty.

Whatever the departmental context, for the interviewing process to be meaningful to researchers themselves and its use credible to reviewers, it is important that researchers understand why they are choosing interviewing rather than experimental or quasi-experimental research. They must understand something about the history of science, the development of positivism, and the critique of positivism as it is applied to the social sciences in general and the field of education in particular.

Because there is currently more acceptance of qualitative research in graduate programs in education, many new researchers have not been asked to learn the assumptions and the practices of experimental or quasi-experimental research. Without this background, qualitative researchers do not know what they do not know about methodology. Consequently, their rationale for choosing a qualitative over a quantitative approach may not be as well grounded as it could be.

At the minimum, Campbell and Stanley's (1963) definitive essay on threats to what they call internal and external validity in experimental and quasi-experimental research should be required reading for all those who intend to do interviewing and other forms of qualitative research. They should grapple firsthand with the issues that shaped a generation of educational researchers and that still inform a significant body of educational research practice today. Even better would be thoughtful reading in the history of science and epistemology. (See, e.g., James, 1947; Johnson, 1975; Lincoln & Guba, 1985; Mannheim, 1975; Matson, 1966; Polanyi, 1958.)

WORKING WITH THE MATERIAL

Research proposals should describe how researchers intend to work with and analyze the material they gather. Describing this process ahead of time is especially difficult for those who are doing empirical research for the first time. It is difficult to project how they will work with material from interview participants if they have never done interviewing work before. In Chapter 8, I discuss working with the material. I stress the importance of paying attention to the words of the participant, using those words to report on the results as much as possible, and looking for both salient material within individual interviews and connections among interviews and participants.

The role that theory plays becomes an issue when researchers are actually trying to analyze and interpret the material they gather. Some scholars would argue that the theory used to discern and forge relationships among the words that participants share with interviewers must come out of those words themselves. Theory cannot and should not be imposed on the words but must emanate from them. This approach, extensively discussed by Glaser and Strauss (1967), has been somewhat persuasive in the field of qualitative research. It argues, rightly I think, especially against taking theoretical frameworks developed in other contexts and force-fitting the words of the participants into the matrices developed from those theories.

On the other hand it may be naïve for us to argue that researchers can be theory free. Everyone has theories. They are the explanations people develop to help them make connections among events. Theories are not the private preserve of scientists. Interviewers walk into interviews with theories about human behavior, teaching and learning, the organization of schools, and the way societies work. Some of the theories are informed and supported by others, and some are idiosyncratic. Others arise from readings interviewers have done in and about the subject of their inquiry.

Some scholars argue that in qualitative research such reading should be kept to a minimum lest it contaminate the view and the understanding of the researcher (Glaser & Strauss, 1967). To a certain extent I agree with that view. It helps to interview participants about their experience if the interviewers are not weighted down with preformed ideas based on what they have gleaned from the literature.

For example, in an interview I had the pleasure of conducting with Linda Miller Cleary in 1996, she spoke to me about the interviewing work that she and her colleague Thomas Peacock were conducting on the experience of American Indian educators (Cleary & Peacock, 1997). She said that, especially when interviewing in a cross-cultural setting, she was cautious about doing too much reading ahead of time. While affirming that she had to do enough reading to be informed and thoughtful about her topic, she was concerned about taking too many stereotypes from the literature into her interviewing. She said that "because I hadn't done a lot of reading, I could ask questions that were real questions" (L. M. Cleary, personal communication, August 11, 1996).

Interviewers must be prepared for their work and be aware of the research on which they are building (Yow, 1994, p. 33). Some researchers go further and argue that interviewers must be expert on their topics before they begin the interviews (Kvale, 1996, p. 147).

I think an intermediate position is sensible at the proposal stage. It is crucial to read enough to be thoughtful and intelligent about the context and history of the topic and to know what literature on the subject is available. It is important to conduct the interviews with that context in mind, while being genuinely open to what the participants are saying. After the interviews have been completed and researchers are starting to work intensively with the material, a return to the reading will help with the analysis and interpretation of the interview material. No prior reading is likely to match the individual stories of participants' experience, but reading before and after the interviews can help make those stories more understandable by providing a context for them.

The range of fields and associated readings that those who do research in education must synthesize is daunting. Often, we fall short of the task. But for those who take the task seriously, it is first-rate intellectual work. This work should be affirmed, represented in the proposal, and digested before the completion of the research, but not necessarily totally before the interviewing. This is a precarious and difficult position to hold. It requires maintaining a delicate balance between the sometimes competing claims of the relevant literature and the experience of the interview participants.

PILOTING YOUR WORK

The best advice I ever received as a researcher was to do a pilot of my proposed study. The dictionary (Gove, 1971) definition of the verb *pilot* is "to guide along strange paths or through dangerous places" (p. 1716).

Although it may not seem ahead of time that the world of interviewing research takes one along strange paths or through dangerous places, the unanticipated twists and turns of the interviewing process and the complexities of the interviewing relationship deserve exploration before the researchers plunge headlong into the thick of their projects.

I urge all interviewing researchers to build into their proposal a pilot venture in which they try out their interviewing design with a small number of participants. They will learn whether their research structure is appropriate for the study they envision. They will come to grips with some of the practical aspects of establishing access, making contact, and conducting the interview. The pilot can alert them to elements of their own interview techniques that support the objectives of the study and to those that detract from those objectives. After completing the pilot, researchers can step back, reflect on their experience, discuss it with their doctoral committee, and revise their research approach based on what they have learned from their pilot experience. (See Locke et al., 2000, pp. 80–82; Maxwell, 1996, for further discussion of pilot studies.)

CONCLUSION

As teachers must plan their objectives and how their methods fit those objectives in order to be responsive to what they meet in their classrooms, so too must researchers plan carefully for research. They must be thoughtful about the what, why, how, who, when, and where of interviewing. They must be as focused and clear as possible about their inquiry when they begin the study. Such planning is the prerequisite for being able to respond thoughtfully and carefully to what emerges as the study proceeds.

Because in-depth interviewing uses a method that is essentially open-ended, preparation, planning, and structure are crucial. Each interview requires a series of instantaneous decisions about what direction to take. Researchers entering an interviewing situation without a plan, sense of purpose, or structure within which to carry out that purpose have little on which to base those decisions. Without a thoughtful structure for their work, they increase the chance of distorting what they learn from their participants (Hyman et al., 1954) and of imposing their own sense of the world on their participants rather than eliciting theirs.

Chapter 4

Establishing Access to, Making Contact with, and Selecting Participants

Before selecting participants for an interview study, the interviewer must both establish access to them and make contact. Because interviewing involves a relationship between the interviewer and the participant, how interviewers gain access to potential participants and make contact with them can affect the beginning of that relationship and every subsequent step in the interviewing process. In this and subsequent chapters, I discuss an idea that I think is equivalent to the First Commandment of interviewing: Be equitable. Respect the participant and yourself. In developing the interviewing relationship, consider what is fair and just to the participant and to you.

THE PERILS OF EASY ACCESS

Beginning interviewers tend to look for the easiest path to their potential participants. They often want to select people with whom they already have a relationship: friends, those with whom they work, students they teach, or others with whom they have some tangential connection. This is understandable but problematic. My experience is that the easier the access, the more complicated the interview.

Interviewing People Whom You Supervise

Conflicts of interest are inherent in interviewing people you supervise. For example, I worked with a doctoral candidate who was the principal of an elementary school. She wanted to interview teachers in her school about their experience in developing collaborative learning projects in their classrooms. She had been deeply involved in the project with her teachers and was eager to understand what effect it had had on their experiences.

In discussions with me, the principal said that her school was small and not a large, unfeeling bureaucracy. She had a close working relationship with the teachers. She felt that they trusted her. Finally, she thought that despite her investment in the project, she could be impartial in the interview.

One of the principles of an equitable interviewing relationship, however, is that the participants not make themselves unduly vulnerable by participating in the interview. In any hierarchical school system, no matter how small, in which a principal has hiring and firing power and control over other working conditions, a teacher being interviewed by the principal may not feel free to talk openly. That is especially the case when the teachers know that the interviewer has an investment in the program. The issue in such cases is not whether the principal can achieve enough distance from the subject to allow her to explore fully, but rather whether the teachers she is interviewing feel secure in that exploration. If they do not, the outcomes of such interviews are not likely to be productive.

As a general principle then, it is wise to avoid interviewing participants whom you supervise (de Laine, 2000, p. 122, and Morse, 1994, p. 27, briefly but compellingly discuss this issue). That does not mean in this case that the doctoral candidate could not explore the experiences of elementary teachers in collaborative learning projects; it does mean that she had to seek to understand the experience of teachers in schools other than her own.

Interviewing Your Students

Inexperienced interviewers who are also teachers often conceptualize a study that involves interviewing students, and they are often sorely tempted to interview their own. As legitimate as it may be to want to understand the effectiveness of, say, a teaching method or a curriculum, a student can hardly be open to his or her teacher who has both so much power and so much invested in the situation. The teacher-researcher should seek to interview students in some other setting with some other teacher who is using a similar method or curriculum.

Interviewing Acquaintances

Sometimes new interviewers want to select participants whom they know but not in a way related to the subject of study. For example, one doctoral candidate was contemplating an interview study about the complexities of being a cooperating teacher for social studies student teachers. He wanted to interview a participant with whom he did not work professionally but with whom he had regular contact at church. Even experienced interviewers cannot anticipate some of the uncomfortable situations that may develop in an interview. Having to consider not only the interviewing relationship but a church relationship as well might limit the full potential of such an interview.

For example, in an interview about the experience of being a cooperating teacher, the acquaintance from church might reveal that the reason he or she takes on student teachers is for the free time it allows. Normally an interviewer would want to follow up on an aspect of an interview that made him or her feel uneasy, but to do so in this case could affect his relationship with the participant at church. The interviewer may avoid a follow-up, slant the follow-up, or in some other way distort the interview process because of concern for his or her other relationship with the participant. The result is either incomplete or distorted information on a key aspect of the subject of study.

Interviewing Friends

Some new interviewers with whom I have worked want to interview participants to whom they have easy access because of friendship. The interviewing relationship in such cases can seldom develop on its own merit. It is affected by the friendship in obvious and less obvious ways.

One of the less obvious ways is that the interviewers and the participants who are friends usually assume that they understand each other. Instead of exploring assumptions and seeking clarity about events and experiences, they tend to assume that they know what is being said. The interviewer and the participant need to have enough distance from each other that they take nothing for granted (see Bell & Nutt, 2002; Bogdan & Taylor, 1975; Hyman et al., 1954; McCracken, 1988; Spradley, 1979).

Taking Oneself Just Seriously Enough

In addition to feeling shy about a process with which they have had little practice (Hyman et al., 1954), a major reason that some doctoral candidates with whom I have worked want to capitalize on easy access is that they tend not to take themselves seriously as researchers. Beginning interviewers find it difficult to imagine asking strangers to spend 4½ hours with them.

Many doctoral candidates see research as something others do. Our educational system is structured so that most people consume research but seldom produce it. This has led many to adopt an uncritical attitude about published material and to regard it as somehow sacred. Doing research is seen as an elite occupation, done only by those at the top of the hierarchy (see Bernstein, 1975).

At the same time, when dissertation research does not grow organically out of the course work, clinical experiences, and independent reading that have gone before, it becomes a requirement to be overcome. Doctoral candidates who have had little practice in doing research and who see it as a hurdle rather than an opportunity find it difficult to affirm their own interest in their subject, their own status as researchers, the power of their research method, or the utility of their work other than to fulfill a requirement.

Cumulative societal inequities can exact a heavy toll on researchers at this juncture. Research in our society has long been seen as a male preserve, especially a White male preserve, associated with class and privilege. New researchers who are not middle-class, White males may have to struggle against social conventions to take themselves seriously in their task. Some doctoral candidates need bracing from their advisors and their peers at this point in their program in order to affirm themselves as researchers. Taking oneself seriously enough as a researcher is a first step toward establishing equity in the interviewing relationship.

ACCESS THROUGH FORMAL GATEKEEPERS

When interviewers try to contact potential participants whom they do not know, they often face gatekeepers who control access to those people. Gatekeepers can range from the absolutely legitimate (to be respected) to the self-declared (to be avoided). If a researcher's study involves participants below the age of 18, for example, access to them must involve absolutely legitimate gatekeepers: the participants' parents or guardians. Although it may be appropriate to seek access to students through the schools, very soon in the process the parents or guardians of the children must affirm that access. Within the schools themselves, teachers, principals, and superintendents serve as legitimate gatekeepers whom researchers must heed.

Some participants are accessible only through the institutions in which they reside or work. For example, if a researcher wanted to interview prisoners about prison education programs, it is not likely that there would be any route of access other than through the warden. (See Code of Federal Regulations, 2001, 45\46.305,306, for regulations regarding research with prisoners.) A researcher studying the experience of people at a particular site, whether it be factory, school, church, human service organization, or business, must gain access through the person who has responsibility for the operation of the site. (See Lincoln & Guba, 1985, p. 252; Richardson et al., 1965, p. 97.)

On the other hand, one researching an experience or a process that takes place in a number of sites, but not studying the workings of any particular site, may not need to seek access through an authority. Such a researcher may want to study the work of high school teachers who teach in many schools scattered through a region or even across the country. In such a case, the researcher might go directly to them without asking for permission from their principals.

Likewise, a researcher studying the experience of students in high school, but not in a particular high school, might not have to seek access through a principal but only through parents. However, in both cases, if a researcher does not seek permission from a principal, the researcher would not be able to interview in the school building itself. In general, the more adult and autonomous the potential participants (for example, prisoners have little autonomy), the more likely that access can be more direct, if a particular site is not the subject of the inquiry.

In our study of community college faculty (Seidman, 1985), my colleagues and I interviewed 76 participants in approximately 25 different community colleges in Massachusetts, New York State, and California. Because we were not studying a particular community college, we did not seek access to individual faculty through the administrators of the colleges. On the other hand, we were never secretive about our work; it would have been difficult to be so, carrying, as we were, a tape recorder large enough to allow us to make audiotapes of a sound quality suitable for the film that we made in the first phase of our research (Sullivan & Seidman, 1982). But even if we had been using a small, pocket-sized tape recorder, we would not have hidden our research from others. When asked in the halls what we were doing at the college, we answered explicitly about our project.

On only one occasion was a faculty member uncomfortable with our approaching him directly and not through his administration. We told him that he should inform the administration of our project and our wish to interview him; we made it clear that we were not doing research about the site. We said that if an administrator wanted to meet with us, we would be happy to do so in order to explain our project, but we were not eager to seek permission from administrators to interview individual faculty. The participant did inform his administration, but no one wanted to meet us.

Sometimes the cooperation of formal gatekeepers may be necessary but fraught with complications. For example, gatekeepers may allow researchers access to employees in their organization and encourage them to participate. Such encouragement could raise the ethical question of how free employees are not to volunteer for the research if their supervisor is encouraging participation (Birch & Miller, 2002, pp. 99–100).

INFORMAL GATEKEEPERS

Sometimes although there is no formal gatekeeper, there is an informal one (Richardson et al., 1965). Most faculties, for example, usually include a few members who are widely respected and looked to for guidance when decisions about whether or not to support an effort are made. In small groups, there is usually at least one person who, without having formal authority, nevertheless holds moral suasion. If that person participates in a project, then it must be okay; if he or she doesn't, then the group feels there must be a good reason for not doing so. To the extent that interviewers can identify informal gatekeepers, not to use them formally for seeking access to others but to gain their participation in the project as a sign of respect for the effort, access to others in the group may be facilitated.

On the other hand, groups often have self-appointed gatekeepers, who feel they must be informed and must try to control everything that goes on, even if they have no formal authority. Their self-importance is not respected by others in the group; avoiding their involvement in the study may be the best way to facilitate access to others in such a group.

ACCESS AND HIERARCHY

One of the differences between research and evaluation or policy studies is that the latter are often sponsored by an agency close to the people who participate in the interviews. In such studies, authority for access to participants often is formally granted by administrators in charge.

There is a sense of official sponsorship of the project (Lincoln & Guba, 1985), which affects the equity of the relationship between interviewer and participant. It is almost as if the interviewer were someone higher in the hierarchy instead of outside it.

Whenever possible, it is important to establish access to participants through their peers rather than through people "above" or "below" them in their hierarchy. For interviewing children, peer access may not be feasible. But in other situations, the demand of equity in the interviewing relationship calls for peer access when possible. If your participants are teachers, for example, try to establish access to them through other teachers; if they are counselors, reach them if at all possible through other counselors.

MAKING CONTACT

Do it yourself. Try not to rely on third parties to make contact with your potential participants. No matter how expedient it seems to have someone else who knows potential participants explain your project to them, try to avoid doing so. Building the interviewing relationship begins the moment the potential participant hears of the study. Third parties may be very familiar with potential participants, but they can seldom do justice to the nature of someone else's project. They have not internalized it the way the researcher has; they do not have the investment in it that the researcher does. Once having introduced the subject, they can seldom respond to questions that naturally might arise. Third parties may be necessary for gaining access to potential participants but should be used as little as possible to make actual contact with them.

A contact visit before the actual interview aids in selecting participants and helps build a foundation for the interview relationship. A contact visit can also convince an interviewer that a good interviewing relationship with a particular potential participant is not likely to develop. The more care and thoroughness interviewers put into making contact, the better foundation they establish for the interviewing relationship.

MAKE A CONTACT VISIT IN PERSON

Telephoning is often a necessary first step in making contact, but if possible it should consist of only a brief introduction, an explanation of how the interviewer gained access to the person's name, and a decision on when to meet. Avoid asking the potential participant for a yes or no answer about participating. An easy "yes" from someone who has not met the interviewer or heard enough about the interviews can backfire later. A "no" that is a defense against too much initial pressure gets the interviewer nowhere (see Richardson et al., 1965, p. 97). The major purpose of the telephone contact is to set up a time when the interviewer and the potential participant can meet in person to discuss the study.

It takes time, money, and effort to arrange a separate contact visit with individual potential participants or even a group, but they are almost always well spent. The purpose of the contact visit is at least threefold. The most important is to lay the groundwork for the mutual respect necessary to the interview process. By taking the time to make a separate contact visit to introduce him- or herself and the study, an interviewer is saying implicitly to the potential participants, "You are important. I take you seriously. I respect my work and you enough to want to make a separate trip to meet with you to explain the project."

Although individual contact visits tend to be more effective, it is possible also to meet with a group of potential participants. Group contact visits save time and wear on the interviewer by allowing one explanation of the study to several people at once. On the downside, one potential participant's skepticism about participating can affect the attitude of others in the group.

Clearly, interviewers will not always be able to make in-person contact and will have to rely on other means, such as the telephone or e-mail. E-mail has become a prominent component of the contact process. Doctoral candidates with whom I work, however, have reported ambiguous results in making initial contact with potential participants by e-mail. With the skepticism that abounds about receiving e-mail from unknown contacts, it is quite easy for a potential participant to disregard an initial contact by e-mail. However, once the contact has been made by an in-person visit, by telephone, or via regular mail, e-mail becomes especially useful in confirming interview appointments, follow-up arrangements, and maintaining contact through the research process.

Whether in person, on the telephone, or in an e-mail message, it is important at this point to present the nature of the study in as broad a context as possible and to be explicit about what will be expected of the participant. Seriousness but friendliness of tone, purposefulness but flexibility in approach, and openness but conciseness in presentation are characteristics that can enhance a contact visit whether conducted in person or on the phone. (For discussions of the importance of the first contact, see Dexter, 1970, p. 34; Hyman et al., 1954, p. 201; Marshall & Rossman, 1989, p. 65.)

The contact visit allows the interviewer to become familiar with the setting in which potential participants live or work before the interview starts. It also allows interviewers to find their way to potential participants so that they are better able to keep their interviewing appointments. In addition to building mutual respect and explaining the nature of the interview study, a second important purpose of the contact visit is to determine whether potential participants are interested. In-depth interviewing asks a great deal of both participants and interviewers. It is no trivial matter to arrange three 90-minute interviews spaced as much as a week apart. It is important that likely participants understand the nature of the study, how they fit into it, and the purpose of the three-interview sequence.

The contact visit also initiates the process of informed consent, which is necessary in most and desirable in almost all interviewing research. (See Chapter 5.) Although I seldom show the informed consent form in the contact visit, I orally go over all aspects of the study and what the consent form covers, so participants will not be surprised by anything included on the form. I usually present the actual form and ask the participant to sign it at the time of the first interview. That is an important time, immediately before I actually start the first interview, to confirm that the participants understand what is involved in their accepting the invitation to be interviewed (Corbin & Morse, 2003, p. 341).

BUILDING THE PARTICIPANT POOL

Another primary purpose of the contact visit is to assess the appropriateness of a participant for the study. The major criterion for appropriateness is whether the subject of the researcher's study is central to the participant's experience. For example, a doctoral candidate wanting to study the way process writing affects an English teacher's experience in teaching writing must select English teachers for whom process writing plays a central role in their teaching.

As the interviewer speaks with potential participants, he or she can keep a record of those who seem most suitable, noting their key characteristics that are related to the subject of the study. Whether the interviewer asks participants to join the study at some point in the contact visit or gets back to them at a later date, he or she must remain aware of the character of the growing participant pool in order to be purposeful in the sampling. (See the section on Selecting Participants later in this chapter.)

SOME LOGISTICAL CONSIDERATIONS

The experience of scheduling a contact visit often reflects what trying to schedule the actual interview with the participant will be like. If one is a reasonable process, the other is likely to be so too. If scheduling one contact visit is unduly frustrating, the interviewer may do well to take that into account in proceeding to build the participant pool.

Because of the time and energy required of both participants and interviewers, every step the interviewer takes to ease the logistics of the process is a step toward allowing the available energy to be focused on the interview itself. To facilitate communication, confirmation of appointments, and follow-up after the interviews, it is important for interviewers to develop a database of their participants. They can use the contact visit to begin to collect data.

A simple participant information form can be of considerable use throughout the study. The form usually has two purposes: to facilitate communication between the interviewer and the participants; and to record basic data about the participant that will inform the final choice of participants and the reporting on the data later in the study. At minimum, the form should include the participants' home and work addresses, telephone numbers, and e-mail address, the best time to be in touch with them, and the time to avoid calling them. Paying attention to the details of communications with participants from the beginning of the interview relationship can help in avoiding the mishaps of missed or confused appointments that can later plague an interview study.

The contact visit can also be used to determine the best times, places, and dates to interview potential participants. These are crucial. The place of the interview should be convenient to the participant, private, yet if at all possible familiar to him or her. It should be one in which the participant feels comfortable and secure. A public place such as a cafeteria or a coffee shop may seem convenient, but the noise, the lack of privacy, and the likelihood of the interview's becoming an event for others to comment upon undermine the effectiveness of such places for interviews.

If it can be determined at the time of the contact visit that a person would be an appropriate participant in the study, the interviewer can schedule time and dates right then. The interviewer should try to let the participant choose the hour, scheduling interviews within a time period consistent with the purpose of the three-interview structure as described in Chapter 2. As pointed out previously, because each interview is meant to build on the preceding one, they are optimally spaced no more than a week and no less than a day apart.

In considering the time, dates, and place of interviews, in addition to considering the safety of the arrangements for both participants and interviewers (Smith, 1992, p. 103), the prevailing principle must be equity. The participants are giving the interviewers something they want. The interviewers must be flexible enough to accommodate the participants' choice of location, time, and date. On the other hand, the interviewers also have constraints. Although equity necessitates flexibility, interviewers must also learn to set up interviews in such a way that they themselves are comfortable with the resulting schedule. Resentment on the part of either participant or interviewer will not bode well ultimately for the interviews.

After the contact visit, interviewers should write follow-up letters to the participants they select and to those they do not. The letters are used to thank the potential participants for meeting with the interviewers and, in the case of those who are selected for the study and who agree to participate, to confirm in writing the schedule of interview appointments.

Such detailed follow-up work in writing may seem onerous to the prospective interviewer; however, equity requires such consideration. In addition, this kind of step-by-step attention can have enormous practical benefits to the interviewer. Few things are more frustrating in an interview study than to drive a few hours to an appointment only to have the participant not show up. Sometimes the no-show is the result of poor communication. Sometimes it reflects a participant's lack of enthusiasm for the process because he or she feels asked to give a great deal while being offered very little consideration in return. In interviewing research, paying attention to the details of access and contact before the interviewing begins is the best investment interviewers can make as they select their participants and prepare to begin the interviews.

SELECTING PARTICIPANTS

Either during the contact process or shortly thereafter the researcher takes the crucial step of selecting the people he or she will interview. The purpose of an in-depth interview study is to understand the experience of those who are interviewed, not to predict or to control that experience. (See Van Manen, 1990, p. 22, for further comment on this fundamental characteristic of a phenomenological approach to research.) Because hypotheses are not being tested, the issue is not whether the researcher can generalize the finding of an interview study to a broader population. Instead the researcher's task is to present the experience of the people he or she interviews in compelling enough detail and in sufficient depth that those who read the study can connect to that experience, learn how it is constituted, and deepen their understanding of the issues it reflects. Because the basic assumptions underlying an interview study are different from those of an experimental study, selecting participants is approached differently.

"Only Connect"

The United States has more than 200,000 community college faculty. In our study of the work of community college faculty (Seidman, 1985), we could interview only 76 of them. The problem we faced was how to select those 76 participants so that what we learned about their experience would not be easily dismissed as idiosyncratic to them and irrelevant to a larger population. In their influential essay on experimental and quasi-experimental design, Campbell and Stanley (1963) call this the problem of external validity.

A conventional way of defining the issue is to ask whether what is learned from the interview sample can be generalized to the larger population. One step toward assuring generalizability is to select a sample that is representative of the larger population. The dominant approach to representativeness in experimental and quasi-experimental studies has been the random selection of participants. Theoretically, if a large enough sample is selected randomly or through a stratified, randomized approach, the resulting participant pool is not likely to be idiosyncratic.

In interview studies, however, it is not possible to employ random sampling or even a stratified random-sampling approach. Randomness is a statistical concept that depends on a very large number of participants. True randomness would be prohibitive in an in-depth interview study. Furthermore, interview participants must consent to be interviewed, so there is always an element of self-selection in an interview study. Self-selection and randomness are not compatible.

The job of an in-depth interviewer is to go to such depth in the interviews that surface considerations of representativeness and generalizability are replaced by a compelling evocation of an individual's experience.

When this experience can be captured in depth, then two possibilities for making connections develop. They are the interview researcher's alternative to generalizability. (See Lincoln & Guba, 1985, for an extensive discussion of the concept of generalization.) First, the researcher may find connections among the experiences of the individuals he or she interviews. Such links among people whose individual lives are quite different but who are affected by common structural and social forces can help the reader see patterns in that experience. The researcher calls those connections to the readers' attention for inspection and exploration.

Second, by presenting the stories of participants' experience, interviewers open up for readers the possibility of connecting their own stories to those presented in the study. In connecting, readers may not learn how to control or predict the experience being studied or their own, but they will understand better their complexities. They will appreciate more the intricate ways in which individual lives interact with social and structural forces and, perhaps, be more understanding and even humble in the face of those intricacies.

Purposeful Sampling

How best to select participants who will facilitate the ability of others to connect if random selection is not an option? The most commonly agreed upon answer is purposeful sampling. Patton's (1989) discussion of purposeful-sampling techniques is very thoughtful. He suggests several approaches, including "typical case," "extreme or deviant case," "critical case," "sensitive case," "convenience" sampling, and "maximum variation" sampling (pp. 100–107).

Maximum variation sampling can refer to both sites and people (Tagg, 1985). The range of people and sites from which the sample is selected should be fair to the larger population. This sampling technique should allow the widest possibility for readers of the study to connect to what they are reading. In my experience maximum variation sampling provides the most effective basic strategy for selecting participants for interview studies.

Consider, for example, a study in which the interviewer wants to explore the experience of minority teachers in local teachers' unions in urban school districts in Massachusetts (Galvan, 1990). Using the maximum variation approach, the researcher would analyze the potential population to assess the maximum range of sites and people that constitute the population.

First she would have to define what she meant by the term *urban*. Then she would have to determine the range of school systems in Massachusetts that fall within her definition. Within those systems she would have to decide whether she was interested in the experience of all minority teachers, those in grades K–12, or just those in some particular grade level.

In Massachusetts, local teachers' unions are usually affiliated with either the National Education Association or the American Federation of Teachers. She would have to decide whether she was interested in studying the experience of minority teachers from both unions or from just one.

After considering the range of sites, she would then have to consider the range of people who are minority teachers and belong to local teachers' unions. She would have to determine the relative number of male and female minority teachers, the range of ethnic groups represented, the range of subject matter they teach, their levels of teaching, and the age and experience of teachers represented in the larger population.

The above characteristics are illustrative but not exhaustive of the range of variations present in the population whose experience this researcher might want to try to understand. If the range became unmanageable, the researcher would want to limit the study, looking at, for example, the experience of one minority group in a number of locals or the experience of the full range of minority members in one or two locals. The goal would remain to sample purposely the widest variation of sites and people within the limits of the study.

In addition to selecting participants who reflect the wide range in the larger population under study, another useful approach is to select some participants who are outside that range and may in some sense be considered negative cases (Lincoln & Guba, 1985; Locke, Silverman, & Spirduso, 2004, pp. 222–223; Weiss, 1994, pp. 29–32). In the study discussed above about what it is like for a minority teacher to be a member of a local teachers' union, it would also be useful to include some nonminority teachers who are also members of the local. If the researcher discovers through interviews that nonminority and minority teachers are having similar experiences, then the researcher will know that some issues may not be a matter of ethnicity or majority-minority status.

As another example, Schatzkamer (1986) was interested in studying the experience of older women returning to community colleges. She also decided to interview some older men who were returning to college to see in what ways their experience connected to that of the women in her sample. Selecting participants to interview who are outside the range of those at the center of the study is an effective way for interviewers to check themselves against drawing easy conclusions from their research.

SNARES TO AVOID IN THE SELECTION PROCESS

New interviewers may take too personally a potential participant's reluctance to get involved. It does little good to try to persuade such a person to participate in an interview she or he would rather not do. In the face of initial reluctance, interviewers may go to great lengths to exercise persuasion only to find later the interview itself to be an ongoing struggle (Richardson et al., 1965). The interviewer must strike a balance between too easily accepting a quick expression of disinterest from a potential participant and too ardently trying to persuade a reluctant one that she or he really should participate.

Another snare is the potential participant who is too eager to be interviewed. During the contact visit an interviewer can ascertain whether the person has some ax to grind. In a contact visit Sullivan and I made to one community college, we learned that the college had just dismissed its president. The school was divided into factions: those who had worked for the president's dismissal and those who had not. Some of the faculty we contacted were very reluctant to get involved in an interview. Others were too eager. The purpose of our study was understanding the work of community college faculty. Although it is true that academic politics are a part of that work, in this particular case the partisan politics of the campus threatened to load our study with interview participants inclined to be more like informers (Dean & Whyte, 1958; Lincoln & Guba, 1985; Richardson et al., 1965).

On occasion during a contact visit, someone would tell us we must interview a colleague who won an award and would be wonderful to talk to. Our instinct was always to avoid such "stars." The method of in-depth interviewing elicits people's stories in a way that shows each person to be interesting no matter how uncelebrated.

HOW MANY PARTICIPANTS ARE ENOUGH?

New interviewers frequently ask how many participants they must have in their study. Some researchers argue for an emerging research design in which the number of participants in a study is not established ahead of time. New participants are added as new dimensions of the issues become apparent through earlier interviews (Lincoln & Guba, 1985; Rubin & Rubin, 1995). Other researchers discuss a "snowballing" approach to selecting participants, in which one participant leads to another (Bertaux, 1981). But even if researchers use a purposeful sampling technique designed to gain maximum variation and then add to their sample through a snowballing process, they must know when they have interviewed enough participants.

There are two criteria for enough. The first is sufficiency. Are there sufficient numbers to reflect the range of participants and sites that make up the population so that others outside the sample might have a chance to connect to the experiences of those in it? In our community college study, we had to have enough participants to reflect vocational and liberal arts faculty; men, women, and minorities; and age and experience ranges. We also considered faculty with advanced degrees and without advanced degrees. In addition, we were reluctant to interview only one person in any particular category.

The other criterion is saturation of information. A number of writers (Douglas, 1976; Glaser & Strauss, 1967; Lincoln & Guba, 1985; Rubin & Rubin, 1995; Weiss, 1994) discuss a point in a study at which the interviewer begins to hear the same information reported. He or she is no longer learning anything new. Douglas (1985) is even bold enough to attempt to assess when that began to happen in his studies. If he had to pick a number, he said, it would be 25 participants.

I would be reluctant to establish such a number. "Enough" is an interactive reflection of every step of the interview process and different for each study and each researcher. The criteria of sufficiency and saturation are useful, but practical exigencies of time, money, and other resources also play a role, especially in doctoral research. On the other hand, if I were to err, I would err on the side of more rather than less. I have seen some graduate students struggle to make sense of data that are just too thin because they did not interview enough participants. Interviewing fewer participants may save time earlier in the study, but may add complications and frustration at the point of working with, analyzing, and interpreting the interview data.

The method of in-depth, phenomenological interviewing applied to a sample of participants who all experience similar structural and social conditions gives enormous power to the stories of a relatively few participants. Researchers can figure out ahead of time the range of sites and people that they would like to sample and set a goal for a certain number of participants in the study. At some point, however, the interviewer may recognize that he or she is not learning anything decidedly new and that the process of interviewing itself is becoming laborious rather than pleasurable (Bertaux, 1981). That is a time to say "enough."

Chapter 5

The Path to Institutional Review Boards and Informed Consent

Many current ethical concerns for the welfare of humans who participate in research studies stem from indignities perpetrated on human research subjects both in Europe and in the United States throughout the 20th century. The World War II Nazi violations of basic human rights in carrying out medical experiments on prisoners in concentration camps are relatively well known. After World War II, the trials of the doctors involved in that research led to the development of the Nuremberg Code. That code, adopted by the United Nations in 1946, established the fundamental, essential ethical principle in research with humans: All participation in such research must be voluntary (Annas, 1992; Reynolds, 1979). (The Nuremberg Code is readily accessible on the Internet by searching its name. Accounts of the trials of concentration camp doctors that led to the Nuremberg Code are also accessible on the Internet. Search for "Nuremberg doctors' trials." Also see Mitscherlich & Mielke, 1949.)

Violations of basic human rights have occurred as well in research in the United States. Of these, the most infamous became known as the Tuskegee Syphilis Experiment, which began in the 1930s and continued for 40 years. So that the researchers could continue to trace the effects of syphilis, antibiotic treatments for the disease were withheld from the study's impoverished African-American participants, after such treatments had become available (Heller, 1972).

THE BELMONT REPORT

Faced with the fact that the disregard for human welfare in research occurred not just abroad but also at home, various departments of the U.S. government issued federal guidelines concerning the protection of the rights of human subjects during the 1950s, 1960s, and 1970s. (See

Anderson, 1996; Applebaum, Lidz, & Meisel, 1987; Faden & Beauchamp, 1986.) In an attempt to bring consistency to the federal effort to protect humans who participate in research, Congress established the National Commission for the Protection of Human Subjects of Biomedical and Behavioral Research in 1974.

After 4 years of deliberation, the Commission produced its influential *Belmont Report: Ethical Principles and Guidelines for the Protection of Human Subjects of Research* (The National Commission for the Protection of Human Subjects of Biomedical and Behavioral Research, 1979). The *Belmont Report* presents clearly what the members of the commission considered to be at stake ethically in research with humans It establishes three basic ethical principles that must be observed in research with human beings:

1. *Respect for Persons:* Respect for individuals' autonomy and the need to protect those whose human condition results in reduced autonomy.
2. *Beneficence:* The Hippocratic imperative to do no harm, and the stricture to maximize benefits and minimize risk when considering research with humans.
3. *Justice:* Research must involve the equitable selection of participants and must be fair to all who participate. Once a positive benefit is discovered, it must be extended to all involved in the research, in contrast to the Tuskegee research.

The *Belmont Report* is easily available on the Internet by searching its name. It is short, lucid, and because it gives the underpinning of subsequent federal regulations in this area, well worth reading.

THE ESTABLISHMENT OF
LOCAL INSTITUTIONAL REVIEW BOARDS

With the *Belmont Report* providing guidance, the federal government began the process of harmonizing the regulations that had been issued by various agencies into what is called the common rule, now adhered to by many federal agencies. The common rule refers to the regulations presented in the Code of Federal Regulations, Title 45, Part 46, Protection of Human Subjects (Protection of Human Subjects, 2001). In print these regulations are often referred to as 45 CFR 46. For a more detailed history of these regulations, see Anderson (1996).

In formulating 45 CFR 46, the government made a key decision to decentralize the process of protecting human subjects of research. The regulations require colleges, universities, hospitals, research institutes, and other organizations that conduct human research and receive federal funding to establish local Institutional Review Boards (IRBs). The local IRB's function is to assure that research done under the auspices of the institution is done with ethical regard to the rights and welfare of human participants. In colleges and universities, the regulations require the local IRB to review and approve all research done with humans, unless after an initial review the IRB itself declares that the research is exempt. The regulations also provide for the possibility that some types of research may be eligible for "expedited" review, that is review by an alternate process rather than by the entire IRB.

IRB Membership and Review Process

IRBs require interviewing researchers to submit their proposed research for review before they begin their project. In the case of doctoral candidates, the IRB review is an additional process separate from the approval of the dissertation proposal by their doctoral committee. The IRB review may seem like an obstacle and may cause anxiety for new researchers. One way to gain confidence and a sense of autonomy in the review process is to read 45 CFR 46 on the "Protection of Human Subjects" (2001). While the regulatory language may initially seem difficult, studying it can assist new researchers to overcome feeling intimidated by the regulations. (Researchers can easily access 45 CFR 46 on the Internet by searching 45 CFR 46.) My own experience is that rather than being an obstacle, an IRB review, when done well, almost always leads researchers to a heightened awareness of important ethical issues embedded in their proposed research.

In universities, IRBs are composed of faculty members knowledgeable about research, at least one representative from outside the university, and administrative staff (Protection of Human Subjects, 2001, 46.107). Each local IRB will have its own application format, but basically IRBs ask researchers to describe briefly the aims of the research, the nature of their participants, their research methodology, the researchers' qualifications to do research, the risks and benefits involved in the research, and how the researchers will obtain informed consent from their potential participants.

Other countries have similar review processes for research with human participants. The Office for Human Research Protections (OHRP) has developed an *International Compilation of Human Subject Research Protections.* The *Compilation* lists the laws, regulations, and guidelines of over 50 countries where research that is funded or supported by the Department of Health and Human Services is conducted. The *Compilation* provides direct web links to each country's key organizations and laws, whenever available. The *Compilation* can be accessed on the OHRP website: *http://www.hhs.gov/ohrp/international/index.html#NatlPol* (OHRP email communication, July 20, 2005). If your research originates in the United States but will be carried out abroad, you will have to comply with your local IRB process *and* your host country's formal review process. Equally important, in some countries, which may or may not have formal review processes, researchers must be sensitive to local cultural expectations of what is ethical (Cleary, 2005).

In 2000 and 2001, two deaths of participants in medical research at prominent United States hospitals made national headlines. Investigations revealed that the participants had not been fully informed about the risks they faced in participating in the research (Kolata, 2001; Stolberg, 2000). Consequently, the federal government has increased its efforts to strengthen the IRB process. Early in their program, doctoral candidates should inquire about their local IRB process. If they plan to do research abroad, they should make early contact with the host country to inquire about its review of research process. They might also see Hubbell (2003) for an excellent description of complexities that may occur when interviewing abroad.

THE INFORMED CONSENT FORM

While there may be some variance in what a local IRB will ask researchers to submit for review, the issue of an informed consent form is almost always pivotal (Ritchie, 2003, p. 217). New interviewers tend to be hesitant about informed consent. They have no doubt of their own good intentions and worry that somehow a formal informed consent process is not congruent with the relationship they envision with their participants. That may lead some new interviewers not to consider or to minimize the risks their research may indeed present (Smith, 1992, p. 102).

In-depth interviewing does not pose the life and death risk of biomedical research, but it is not risk free. Interviewers following the model described in this book may meet with participants three times as they ask them to reconstruct their life histories, provide details of their experiences in particular areas of inquiry, and then reflect on the meaning of those experiences. In the process of this interview sequence, a measure of intimacy can develop between interviewers and participants. That intimacy may lead participants to share aspects of their lives that may cause discomfort and even some degree of emotional distress during the interview process. If, when they write their reports, researchers misuse the words of their participants, the researchers could leave their participants vulnerable to embarrassment and loss of reputation. Participants have the right to be protected against vulnerability in the process of the interviews and in how researchers share the results of the interviews (Kelman, 1977). Informed consent is the first step towards minimizing the risks participants face when they agree to be interviewed.

As expressed in the Nuremberg Code, the essential ethical principle of research with humans is that participants freely volunteer to participate in the research. In order to willingly consent in the truest sense, potential participants must know enough about the research to be able to gauge in a meaningful way whether they want to proceed. Meeting this standard is the underlying logic of the informed consent form.

The federal guidelines for informed consent (Protection of Human Subjects, 46.116–117) were designed primarily with the risks and benefits of biomedical research in mind. Consequently the guidelines have stipulations that are appropriate for experimental research using human subjects, but benefit from adaptation when applied to qualitative research. (For a thoughtful presentation of the fit between the federal guidelines and qualitative research, see Cassell, 1978.) In the discussion below, I have adapted the requirements for informed consent, as they would be applicable to in-depth interviewing research.

EIGHT MAJOR PARTS OF INFORMED CONSENT

A consent form adapted to in-depth interviewing should cover eight major parts:

1. *An invitation to participate in what, to what end, how, how long, and for whom?* The first part of an informed consent form should state explicitly that the potential participant is being invited to take part in a research study. This introduction would be followed with a brief statement of the purpose of the research, how it will be conducted, for how long, and whether there are any sponsors of the research.

2. *Risks*: The second part should outline the potential risks of vulnerability or discomfort for the participant that might result from taking part in the research.
3. *Rights*: The third part should outline the rights of the participants. These rights are designed to mitigate the risks of vulnerability and discomfort and should include an explicit statement that participation in the research is voluntary and that refusal to participate would carry no penalty.
4. *Possible benefits*: The fourth part of the informed consent form would modestly outline the possible benefits of the study in general and for the participant in particular.
5. *Confidentiality of records*: This fifth part should outline the steps the researcher will take to make sure the participant's identity is kept confidential and the extent to which that confidentiality might be limited.
6. *Dissemination*: The sixth part should indicate how the researcher intends to disseminate the results of the research, and seek explicit release for the extensive use of the participant's words in, for example, a dissertation, book, article, or presentation.
7. *Special conditions for children*: In this seventh part, the researcher should stipulate that for children under 18, a parent or guardian must consent for the child to participate.
8. *Contact information and copies of the form*: The final part clarifies how to contact the researcher and the local IRB if participants have questions about their rights or anything else about the research project. In addition, researchers must assure that they have written the form in language that the potential participant is able to comprehend fully.

I have resisted the temptation to replicate a sample of an informed consent form. Since local IRBs have considerable autonomy within federal guidelines, they will develop their own template for researchers to follow. In addition, I think merely copying an example could lead a researcher into trouble. I urge doctoral candidates and other researchers to grapple with the logic of each of the parts of an informed consent form. They then can develop a written consent form based on their understanding of the purpose of each part, the particulars of their research project, and the expectations of their IRB. In my experience, doing so leads to researchers' better internalizing the ethical issues involved and improving how they conduct their research. In what follows, I discuss in more depth issues embedded in each of the eight major parts of the consent form as they apply to in-depth interviewing research.

1. WHAT, HOW LONG, HOW, TO WHAT END, AND FOR WHOM?

What, How Long, and How?

In this section of Part 1, researchers must present briefly, without jargon, what they are asking of the participants. For an in-depth interviewing research project, researchers should state that they are inviting potential participants to take part in interviewing research on the agreed upon topic and that the process involves three separate interviews: the first on their life history, the second on the details of their experience in the area being studied, and the third on the meaning to them of their experience. The interviews will last 90 minutes each, spaced normally over a week or two. Furthermore, researchers must inform participants that their interviews will be audio-taped (see Part 5 below).

To What End?

In this section, researchers briefly explain both the intellectual and instrumental purposes of their research. First, they address why they are studying the particular topic. Second, if researchers are doctoral candidates, for example, they should indicate that they intend to use the research for their dissertations.

For Whom?

Participants should know the full identity of the interviewer. For example, if an interviewer is both an employee of the school district in which he or she is interviewing and a doctoral candidate at a university, both parts of this identity should be stated.

Participants should be told explicitly with whom their recorded words or transcripts might be shared before publication of the study. For example, if students in a school were being interviewed, would the teachers or principal be allowed to see the transcripts? Will the doctoral committee chair have access to the audiotapes?

Finally, if the study is sponsored in any way, that sponsorship should be made clear to participants. For example, a school system may be sponsoring the research, or a granting agency may be funding the research. The interviewer has an obligation to inform the participant of the nature of the sponsorship, if any.

2. RISKS, DISCOMFORTS, AND VULNERABILITY

This section should inform potential participants of risks they might be taking by participating in the research. There are at least two types of risk: risks during the interviews, and risks after the interviews have been completed. (See Corbin & Morse, 2003, for an excellent discussion of such risks.) As pointed out earlier, the process of in-depth interviewing may bring up areas that cause emotional discomfort for the participant. Depending on the potential sensitivity of the topic of study, the researcher should indicate that the process of the interviews could cause discomfort at times and that the researcher will work to minimize such occasions.

Furthermore, when researchers use extensive portions of their participants' words in research reports, it is possible that the participants would become recognizable. If participants' identities were to become known, the public exposure of aspects of their lives they consider private may cause them embarrassment. They may feel that a researcher, by publicly sharing private or deeply personal aspects of their lives, has injured their dignity (Kelman, 1977).

The Oral History Association has developed principles, standards, and guidelines for those doing oral history interviewing which I recommend to readers' attention (Oral History Association, 2004; and Oral History Association, 1992). Its seventh principle states: "Interviewers should guard against possible exploitation of interviewees." Researchers must consider what steps they can take to reduce the threat of exploiting their participants or making them vulnerable.

3. RIGHTS OF THE PARTICIPANT

One important precaution that researchers can take to minimize the risks to participants is to identify the rights that participants have when they take part in research. This part of the consent form serves to inform participants of their rights and indicates the researchers' commitment to abide by them. These rights include, but are not limited, to the following:

Voluntary Participation

Participation in research must be completely voluntary. Therefore, the most fundamental right of the potential participant is not to participate. If a participant chooses not to participate in research, such a choice cannot be prejudicial to the participant. For example, if a researcher is doing research in a classroom, students (and their parents) have a right to say that they will not participate. Their choosing not to participate can in no way affect the students' progress or grade in the class. If they do choose to participate, it must be a decision based on their being fully informed about the study.

Right to Withdraw

Research participants have the right to drop out of a study at any time. The three 90-minute interviews are designed to build a framework for a relationship between the interviewer and the participant that is equitable and leads to a reasonable level of trust between the two. The interview process may lead a participant to divulging information that he or she later regrets having shared (Kirsch, 1999). The participant may become uncomfortable with the interview process and want to withdraw. The researcher must make clear that the participant has the right to withdraw from the study at any time during the interviews and within a specified time after they are completed and before publication of the interview material.

Right of Reviewing and Withholding Interview Material

Short of completely withdrawing from the study, participants have the right to request that material from their interviews be withheld. To exercise that right fully, participants must have the right to review their interviews before they are published.

What right the participant has to review and approve the way the interviewer has worked with the material gathered in the study is less well defined. Interviewers must give participants access to the audiotapes and to the transcripts if requested. Interviewers may share with participants the ways they have worked with individual participant's interview material and how they have analyzed and interpreted that particular material when writing up the study. Finally, interviewers may offer to share the entire report before publication or the parts of the final report that most concern a participant.

Some qualitative researchers consider this step to be crucial for the credibility of the study (Lincoln & Guba, 1985). In the interview work I have done, I have often developed extensive profiles of the participants crafted in their own words from the interview transcripts. When I have done so, I contact the person and offer to share the profile with her or him before I disseminate it. If the participant asks to review the profile, I send it. I inform the participant that I want to know if it contains anything inaccurate or unfair to the larger interview. I also want to know if there is anything in the profile with which the participant is uncomfortable.

Although at this stage I would not disseminate anything that a participant told me would make him or her vulnerable, neither would I give the person automatic censure on matters of interpretation. One participant in our community college study asked me to delete a portion of the profile I had developed of him. In the interview, he had said that he was not proud of working at his community college. I agreed to delete the passage to which he was referring because he felt that it could make him vulnerable if he were identified. But later in an interpretive section of the study that was not tied to any single participant, I discussed the issue of community college faculty members' sense of status in their jobs, keeping what that participant had told me in mind.

At some point the interviewer has to become responsible for what he or she writes. In this instance, I felt somewhat compromised in taking that responsibility because the participant had asked me to delete important information that had informed part of my analysis. On the other hand, I was committed to preserving the dignity of participants and not making them vulnerable as a result of their participation in the study. As in many other aspects of interviewing research, the researcher has to balance conflicting claims. The interviewer must be willing to take ownership of the material and be responsible for the consequences. I do not think the researcher can shift the burden of that responsibility to the participant, and yet the participant has an interest in how the researcher carries it out.

Whatever the interviewer decides to do about the participant's rights of review, the most important point is to be explicit about those rights. This is equally important when handling issues of remuneration, discussed in Part 6. Disputes between participants and researchers result more often from their being unclear about the framework within which they are working than from any decision on a specific issue. (For an interesting discussion of the need for clarity and the consequences of confusion in this area, see Lightfoot, 1983.)

The Right to Privacy

The participant has the right to privacy and the right to request that identities remain confidential and not be revealed. The standard assumption in in-depth interviewing research is that participants will remain unidentified. That assumption has implications for interviewers from the moment they start their research. In their proposals, for instance, which are usually public documents, they should avoid listing names of sites or people that could be traced later when the research is completed.

Researchers working with interview material cannot absolutely guarantee confidentiality of identity. The focus of the research is the experience of the participants within the context of their lives. Because a considerable part of that experience may be shared in the research report, a reader who knows the participant may recognize him or her.

Nonetheless, the interviewer can work to protect the identity of the participant and can say how that will be done in the written consent form. For example, the participant has the right to know who will transcribe the interview audiotapes. If it is not to be the interviewer, the interviewer should outline what steps will be taken to assure that the transcriber does not misuse information about the participant. In addition, the participant should be assured that transcriptions will contain only initials for all proper names, so that even if a casual reader were somehow to see the transcripts, no proper names would be present. Third, the interviewer should promise to use pseudonyms in the final report. Fourth, in some cases the interviewer can choose to actively disguise the participant's identity.

In her study, *The Contextual Realities of Being a Lesbian Physical Educator: Living in Two Worlds*, Woods (1990) was concerned that her participants would be vulnerable if they could be identified. As part of her written consent form, she made the following statement and outlined the steps that she would take to protect—but not guarantee—her participants' anonymity:

In a study of this nature, the anonymity of participants is a priority. Although anonymity cannot be fully guaranteed, the following are steps taken at each stage of the research process to protect your anonymity.

A. Access to participants has been gained in two ways: (a) my personal contacts; and (b) contacts given by those being interviewed. All initial contacts with a potential participant will be made by the person or participant suggesting the teacher to be interviewed. I will contact the potential participant directly only if she has agreed to discuss the possibility of being interviewed.

B. All interviews will take place in a safe space to be designated by the participant.

C. The researcher will not interview more than one teacher employed in a single district.

D. With the exception of the dissertation committee chairperson, I will not discuss with the dissertation committee or anyone else any names, teaching locations, or identifying particulars of the participants.

E. Interview transcripts may be completed by two persons: (a) myself; and\or (b) a reputable and discreet transcriber. If someone other than myself transcribes the audiotapes, I will erase from the audiotapes all names and identifying particulars before submitting them for transcription.

F. As stated, pseudonyms will be substituted in the transcripts for all names of persons, schools, school districts, cities, towns, and counties. Every step will be taken to adequately disguise the participant's identity and teaching location in any published materials or presentations.

G. The transcripts will remain in the direct physical possession of the researcher. All audiotapes and consent forms are kept in a safety deposit box. Tapes will be destroyed upon acceptance of the dissertation or, at your request, will be returned to you. (p. 224)

Woods felt that her participants would be taking risks by participating in her study. To protect them and to establish conditions in which they would feel safe to talk, she devised the most effective and practical means she could to minimize those risks. Although I was concerned about her promise to destroy the audiotapes of the interviews, the care she took to protect her participants' identity without guaranteeing them anonymity, and her explicitness with potential participants, seemed to me a model of forthrightness. Recently, the New York Times reported that an East Texas town's school board dismissed the coach of their championship high school girls' basketball team, allegedly because she was a lesbian (Macur, 2005). Such contemporary episodes indicate that the carefulness

Woods exercised in the 1990s to protect the identity of her participants is still warranted.

As Woods indicates, if the likelihood of a participant's being identified is high, and if being so identified would make him or her vulnerable, it may be best to disguise the person's identity. This measure, which is more active than giving the participant a pseudonym, might involve changing the location in which the person resides or the specific nature of the activity being discussed. For example, in *In the Words of the Faculty* (Seidman, 1985), I changed the state in which one participant taught as well as the subject she taught. The guidelines the researcher must use in judging the appropriateness of such changes are whether the likelihood of participants' being identified is high, whether they would be made vulnerable if identified, and whether disguises can be effected in ways that do not distort the data.

Informed consent assumes but does not require that the participant will not be identified (Reynolds, 1979). What it does require is that the participants be informed before the interviews begin as to what steps, if any, will be taken to protect their identity. Mishler (1986) argues that anonymity is not automatically a good thing and that participants should be given the choice as to whether they wish their names to be used. My experience leads me to suggest that interviews be conducted under the assumption that the interviewer will take steps to protect the anonymity of the participants. After the interview is completed, the participants will be in a better position to judge whether they wish to conceal their identities.

4. POSSIBLE BENEFITS

This part of the form should briefly describe both the potential benefits to the participant and to others that might reasonably be expected as a result of the research. The researcher should devise a reasonably modest statement of benefits that will not raise undue expectations, not seem egotistical, and yet justify the risk that usually is present in in-depth interview situations. It is better to promise less than more. Any monetary benefits could be included in the section on dissemination and the ownership of research materials (Part 6).

If interviews are done well, just being listened to may be beneficial to participants. But that type of benefit is more appropriately realized by the participant at the conclusion of the interview than stipulated by the researcher at the beginning.

Benefits to people other than the participants may be real, but also intangible. As researchers we hope to better understand the subject of our inquiry and to share that understanding as a possible contribution to the field and those affected by it. One does not want to overstate the case. It might be best for researchers to say something modest about what they hope to learn as a result of their research and how that learning might possibly benefit the field (L. Hick, personal communication, April 15, 2005).

5. CONFIDENTIALITY OF RECORDS

I have often seen drafts of written consent forms in which interviewers promise that the material they gather will be kept confidential. Keeping material "confidential" means no one sees it other than the interviewer. Such a promise is inconsistent with the purpose and method of in-depth interviewing research. Most people who interview do so because they want to make the experience of individuals accessible to others. They want to share the material they gathered from their participants to a wider audience, not keep it "confidential." When researchers and IRBs use the term *confidential* in interviewing studies, they should be referring to maintaining the confidentiality of the name of the participants who are the source of the records, tapes, and transcripts and any other material that could identify the participants in our research (R. Zussman, personal communication, December 2004).

As indicated in Part 3 on "rights," researchers must take steps to code the identity of their participants from the beginning of the process, so that, for instance, a casual observer happening to see a transcript on a desk could not identify the participant. Original records such as contact-information sheets, informed consent forms, and audiotapes, must be kept in a secure place to guard against the names of participants being accidentally revealed.

Limits to Confidentiality: The Subpoena and Mandated Reporter Requirements

Two major caveats, however, must be raised concerning the confidentiality of records. First, research information is not privileged and is thereby subject to subpoena by the courts (Nejelski & Lerman, 1971; O'Neil, 1996; Reynolds, 1979). Having one's transcripts or tapes subpoenaed could put researchers in conflict with their ethical responsibility to their participants as outlined in the first of the Principles of Professional Responsibility of the American Anthropological Association (1983):

> In research, anthropologists' paramount responsibility is to those they study. When there is a conflict of interest, these individuals must come first. Anthropologists must do everything in their power to protect the physical, social, and psychological welfare and to honor the dignity and privacy of those studied. (p. 1)

When we were doing our study of community college faculty, we interviewed a number of students to understand how their experience related to what the faculty were telling us (Schatzkamer, 1986). In one of the interviews, a student revealed that he occasionally sold drugs on the campus. We were faced with a dilemma. Although it was not likely to happen, this particular person might be arrested, and our interview data could have been subpoenaed and used against him. Though we did not condone his selling marijuana on the campus, we would not have known of it through any way other than our interviews. We did not feel that we could ethically continue to interview him, if those interviews might affect him adversely later. As interesting as his perspective was, we decided that the best course of action was to terminate the interviews and destroy the tapes. It was not an altogether comfortable resolution. But at the time the decision had to be made, we could envision a situation in which our promises of confidentiality could not be honored, and we would not be able to maintain our ethical obligation to the welfare of the participant. (See Yow, 1994, pp. 93–95, for an excellent discussion of this type of issue.)

A second limit to confidentiality would be invoked if during the course of an interview the interviewer hears of the abuse or neglect of a child. In approximately 18 states in the United States, any person, including a researcher, is considered a mandated reporter for child abuse and would be required to report such cases to the appropriate authorities (American Humane Fact Sheet, 2005). Consequently, if researchers' subjects of inquiry are connected to young children, they should indicate in their informed consent forms their obligation to report cases of abuse. The American Humane Fact Sheet (2005) reports that state laws regarding child abuse reporting vary and are revised often. They urge that anyone concerned consult local child protection agencies about relevant state law. Other types of abuse may be subject to mandated reporting as well. Abuse of the elderly requires reporting in many states. In

New Hampshire, in addition to child abuse, an interviewer who learns of mistreatment of an incapacitated adult, student hazing, or of an injury caused by a criminal act would be required to report that information (University of New Hampshire, 2004). Depending on one's research topic and the particular requirements of the state in which the research is being conducted, researchers must caution their participants regarding the limits to confidentiality and the risk this might conceivably mean for the participant.

6. DISSEMINATION

Joint Ownership of Research Material

Valerie Raleigh Yow (1994) has an excellent chapter about the ethics and legalities of interviewing, especially as they apply to the informed consent process. She takes the position (at least partially based on Hirsch, 1982) that the copyright law of 1976 establishes that the moment the researcher shuts off the tape recorder, the tape belongs jointly to both the participant and the researcher. Joint ownership means that the researcher must secure from the participant an explicit release to use the interview material as the researcher plans to use it. The researcher may either draw up a separate release form (see Yow, 1994) or may include in this section of the consent form a clear statement that by signing the consent form, the participants are giving permission to the researcher to use their words in the ways described in the form.

The Extensive Use of Interview Data

Another aspect of the researcher's plans that should be made clear to the participant is the extent to which the researcher might use the material from the interview. In Chapter 8, I discuss ways of working with the material and disseminating it. Suffice it to say here that the intent of this type of interviewing is to use the words of the participants as much as possible to illuminate the experience they are reconstructing in their interviews.

In reporting on in-depth interviewing, researchers often use lengthy excerpts from interview transcripts, whereas many participants imagine that only short quotations will be used from their interviews. In order for participants to give *informed* consent, interviewers must make clear how extensively they plan to use their participants' own words in the final report of the research.

Possible Uses of Interview Data

I suggest to doctoral candidates that they cast the widest net possible in outlining in the consent form the various uses they will make of information collected. On first instinct, many students limit the list of intended uses to their dissertation. This means that if they later decide to publish something from their dissertation or to present their research at a conference, they will then be obligated to go back to their participants to seek additional permission to use the material in ways not originally listed in the consent form. Even though when they are beginning their research, writing such articles or making presentations based on their interviewing may seem like a remote possibility, researchers are well–advised to let their potential participants know of that possibility in the consent form.

Remuneration

Whether the participant can expect any remuneration for participating in the interviews is a major issue that should be explicitly addressed in the consent form. Such remuneration could range from payment for each interview to the promise that if the interviews lead to commercial publication, the participant would have the right to some portion of the royalties. Establishing an equitable percentage of royalties to allocate to participants is difficult, and except in the case of a best-seller, royalties are likely to be very small. If paying per interview, setting the level of compensation can be tricky. Anything more than a token payment could bias potential participants' motivation for taking part in the study. On the other hand, some see the use of peoples' words without paying them as exploitative (Patai, 1987).

In the studies I have conducted with colleagues, we have not offered remuneration to the participants. At the conclusion of an interview, we normally present a token of our appreciation. I think there are other levels of reciprocity that occur in the interview process that can substitute for financial remuneration. Participants have told us that the occasion of their interview was the first time anyone had ever sat down to talk about their work with them. Participants have said that they appreciated being listened to and that participating in the interviews was an important experience for them.

Interviewers have to figure out for themselves the issue of remuneration. Whatever they decide should be stated explicitly in the written consent form. The governing principle should be to give the participant the opportunity to join or not to join the study on the basis of explicit written information in the consent form. It should state clearly that either the participant is agreeing not to make any financial claim upon the interviewer or should state what the basis of the remuneration will be. An unclear position about the issue of money will cause more problems than a clear decision either to remunerate or not.

7. SPECIAL CONDITIONS FOR CHILDREN

If participants have not attained the legal age of consent to treatments or procedures involved in research (age 18 in most jurisdictions), interviewers must obtain the informed consent of a parent or legal guardian. If appropriate, researchers should seek the "assent" of the child, but must obtain the "permission" of a parent or guardian. In cases with "greater than minimal risk" and little direct benefit to the participant, both parents and each guardian must give permission (Protection of Human Subjects, 2001, 46.402, 46.408).

8. CONTACT INFORMATION AND COPIES OF THE FORM

Participants must be able to contact the researcher before, during, and after the interviews are completed. The last part of the consent form should include information about how to contact the researcher in case the participant has questions or concerns about the research. The information should include more than just an e-mail address, since not all participants will have access to e-mail. Many IRBs instruct researchers also to list contact information for their IRB in the event that participants have questions about their rights as participants in the research.

Both participants and researcher should sign the consent form and the researcher should provide a copy for participants as well as keeping one for their research files. An IRB may waive the requirement for the participant to sign the informed consent form if that signature would provide the only record linking the participant and the research and there would be a significant risk to the participant if he or she were identified (Protection of Human Subjects, 2001, 45. 46.117 [c]). Other methods of documenting that informed consent was obtained can be developed with the approval of the IRB.

Appropriate Language

The consent form must be written in language free of jargon. If the participant cannot fully comprehend English, the consent form should be written in the language the participant is able to comprehend most effectively. The process by which researchers present informed consent forms to participants is as crucial as the language of the form. Researchers must talk the consent form through with potential participants to assure that they understand what is written on the form. Neither researchers nor participants can afford to be casual about making sure that the form is understood. But it is the researchers' responsibility to move potential participants beyond a superficial reading of the informed consent form to a thoughtful consideration of it.

THE COMPLEXITIES OF AFFIRMING THE IRB REVIEW PROCESS AND INFORMED CONSENT

When guidelines for seeking informed consent were first issued by federal agencies in the 1960s and 1970s, some researchers felt that the costs of the new procedures outweighed the benefits. Experienced social scientists questioned the emphasis on written informed consent especially for participant observation studies that may be fluid, unfixed, and therefore difficult ones in which to seek explicit consent (Thorne, 1980).

In a response to the first edition of this book, sociologist Kathy Charmaz commented that, although informed consent seems to work well when interviewing professionals, when interviewing working-class participants, she had found that the informed consent form causes many to "feel uncomfortable and sets a suspicious tone to the interview" (personal communication, March 5, 1992). In further discussion of the issue, Charmaz (personal communication, March 23 & 30, 1997) indicated that despite her attempts to use a form that was short, clear, and devoid of jargon, the process of asking the participant to sign the form sometimes contributed to establishing a sense of authority and dominance in the interviewing relationship. I recognize that feeling in my work. When a participant signs the written consent form, I feel a sense of having gotten what I need to proceed and a small measure of control that comes with that accomplishment.

Richard G. Mitchell, Jr.'s (1993) monograph, *Secrecy and Fieldwork,* critiques the easy substitution of the form of ethical procedure for the substance of ethical responsibility on the part of the researcher. That responsibility, according to Mitchell, is to understand and report as fully as possible the experience and the social world of our participants from their perspective. Mitchell also points out that the requirement to seek informed consent protects the weak and the powerful alike. He argues that in some instances, such as his research on "survivalists," fieldwork carried out in secret, with no pretense of seeking informed consent, is necessary if the researcher hopes to gain the essential understanding of the participants he or she may be studying.

Mitchell's perspective is provocative and useful. Doctoral candidates with whom I have worked have indicated that the approach to interviewing I describe in this book can be problematic, for example, when interviewing elites and others in positions of power. (See the discussion of interviewing elites in Chapter 7.) Such participants may either refuse to sign the consent form or, having signed the consent form, take other steps to avoid giving real insight into their perspectives.

There are other situations and settings in which the necessity to seek informed consent may hinder the interviewing process, at least initially (K. Charmaz, personal communication, March 23, 1997). In situations in which participants feel vulnerable because of the sensitive nature of the topic of the interview, they may hesitate to sign the consent form. Participants who, for a range of reasons, have a distrust of forms and formalistic language may balk at being asked to sign. Participants who feel the power relationship between them and the interviewer is inequitable may feel uneasy and awkward when asked to review and sign the form. Interviewing in cross-cultural settings may provide additional complexities for the process of informed consent (Cleary, 2005).

My experience is that the interviewer can deal with some of this uneasiness by thoughtfulness and care in the process of going over the form with the participant. In addition, the process of interviewing the participant three times and developing and sustaining a relationship over a period of time can relieve initial discomfort and can assuage the suspicion that may have arisen at the time that the researcher asked the participant to sign the informed consent form. In circumstances in which the interviewer does not have the ability to build a relationship over time, the informed consent process may be inhibiting. While designed to foster equity between the interviewer and the participant, it may at times inhibit it.

Some social science researchers, arguing for academic freedom of inquiry, bristle at the bureaucratic approach to ethical issues represented by the IRB review process. They insist that the risks inherent in most social science research are in no way comparable to the risks of biomedical research, which the guidelines were primarily designed to address. They assert that the IRB process serves to protect the institution rather than the research participant. (For an early version of this critique, see Douglas, 1979.)

In 2003, in the limited area of oral history, the federal Office for Human Research Protection (OHRP), which is responsible for administering 45 CFR 46, decided that oral history interviewing does not involve the type of research defined by the Department of Health and Human Services regulations and is therefore excluded from Institutional Review Board oversight (L. Shopes, personal communication, October 2004). Since the decision, ambivalence about it has been expressed in many quarters (Brooks, 2005). For a fuller discussion of the oral history exemption from IRB review and the exact wording of the decision, readers may access the Oral History Association homepage on the Internet by searching for the name of the organization. Perhaps most important to note, however, is that most oral historians support the notion of informed consent, with or without the IRB review.

My sense is that while life and death may not be at stake in educational and social science research, the risks to participants are not trivial. The IRB review and informed consent requires that interviewers think through the structure and processes of their study, making them explicit not only to their participants but also to themselves. Developing a satisfactory written consent form requires that interviewers be clear about their purposes, methods, and relationship with their participants. In addition to allowing the potential participant to decide whether to participate in the study on the basis of sufficient information, the informed consent form can also protect interviewers in cases of misunderstanding. The process of making an informed consent form clear can lead a researcher to a more equitable relationship with participants and to the increased effectiveness that almost always flows from equity.

Over time, I expect that more IRBs will have members who are familiar with the assumptions and methods of qualitative research. The give and take between interviewing researchers and IRBs should serve to educate both researchers and IRB members. When an IRB review is done well, that is to say more as an educational process and less as a bureaucratic review (J. Simpson, personal communication, June 2004), it can serve both research participants and researchers well. For all of us involved in this type of research, it is essential to point out that the IRB review process and informed consent is a beginning and not the end of our ethical responsibilities to our participants (McKee, 2004).

Chapter 6

Technique Isn't Everything, But It Is a Lot

I t is tempting to say that interviewing is an art, a reflection of the personality of the interviewer, and cannot be taught. This line of thinking implies that either you are good at it or you are not. But that is only half true. Researchers can learn techniques and skills of interviewing. What follows is a discussion of those skills as I have come to understand them from my own experience of interviewing and that of others.

LISTEN MORE, TALK LESS

Listening is the most important skill in interviewing. The hardest work for many interviewers is to keep quiet and to listen actively. Many books about interviewing concentrate on the types of questions that interviewers ask, but I want to start this chapter by talking about the type of listening the interviewer must do.

Interviewers must listen on at least three levels. First, they must listen to what the participant is saying. They must concentrate on the substance to make sure that they understand it and to assess whether what they are hearing is as detailed and complete as they would like it to be. They must concentrate so that they internalize what participants say. Later, interviewers' questions will often flow from this earlier listening.

On a second level, interviewers must listen for what George Steiner (1978) calls "inner voice," as opposed to an outer, more public voice. An outer, or public, voice always reflects an awareness of the audience. It is not untrue; it is guarded. It is a voice that participants would use if they were talking to an audience of 300 in an auditorium. (For a very thoughtful explication of listening for inner voice, see Devault, 1990, pp. 101–105.)

There is a language of the outer voice to which interviewers can become sensitive. For example, whenever I hear participants talk about the problems they are facing as a "challenge" or their work as an "adventure," I sense that I am hearing a public voice, and I search for ways to get to the inner voice. *Challenge* and *adventure* convey the positive aspects of a participant's grappling with a difficult experience but not the struggle. Another word that attracts my attention is *fascinate*. I often hear that word on talk-show interviews; it usually works to communicate some sort of interest while covering up the exact nature of that interest. Whenever I hear a participant use *fascinate*, I ask for elucidation. By taking participants' language seriously without making them feel defensive about it, interviewers can encourage a level of thoughtfulness more characteristic of inner voice.

On a third level, interviewers—like good teachers in a classroom—must listen while remaining aware of the process as well as the substance. They must be conscious of time during the interview; they must be aware of how much has been covered and how much there is yet to go. They must be sensitive to the participant's energy level and any nonverbal cues he or she may be offering. Interviewers must listen hard to assess the progress of the interview and to stay alert for cues about how to move the interview forward as necessary.

This type of active listening requires concentration and focus beyond what we usually do in everyday life. It requires that, for a good part of the time, we quash our normal instinct to talk. At the same time, interviewers must be ready to say something when a navigational nudge is needed.

In order to facilitate active listening, in addition to tape-recording the interview, interviewers can take notes. These working notes help interviewers concentrate on what the participant is saying. They also help to keep interviewers from interrupting the participant by allowing them to keep track of things that the participant has mentioned in order to come back to these subjects when the timing is right.

A good way to gauge listening skills is to transcribe an interview tape. Separate the interviewer's questions from the participant's responses by new paragraphs. Compare the relative length of the participant's paragraphs with the interviewer's. If the interviewer is listening well, his or her paragraphs will be short and relatively infrequently interspersed among the longer paragraphs of the participant's responses.

Note the following one-page transcript, for example. It is taken from the beginning of interview number two on the experience of being an instructional designer.

> INTERVIEWER: Could you tell me as much as possible about
> the details of your experience at work as an instructional

designer presently or as a grad student working in the area
of instructional design?

PARTICIPANT: The details of instructional design . . . OK

INTERVIEWER: Your present experience . . .

PARTICIPANT: Yeah.

INTERVIEWER: As an instructional designer.

PARTICIPANT: Umh . . . So something like . . . you mean
something like perhaps the last several jobs I've done?

INTERVIEWER: No, what you're presently doing, like as a student
maybe right now or you said you did have a job that you're
working on.

PARTICIPANT: Yeah, well, I have one current, current job, umh,
the thing is that when you said current I may or may in
any given day, I may or may not happen to have a job;
you know they just, they just fall out of the sky. You don't
really—My experience in getting work has been that—no
matter what I do to try to get work I don't see any direct
results between those efforts and getting the jobs, right. On
the other hand, I do get jobs. They just fall out of the sky
[laugh]. All I can say about you know like meteorites. Unh,
and they range over a wide, wide variety of—of contact.
Umh [sniffle] it could be teaching office workers how to use
software. I've done all of those, all of those kinds of things.
Umh, and typically the things start through the proposal,
umh less and less I've been doing the actual proposals, but
usually I'm not ah—the actual getting the business is not
my job and somewhere there is a line between; writing the
proposal is part of getting the business and um so I usually
have something to do with writing the proposal but I don't
do a lot of getting the business. Umh [sniffle] somewhere
after the proposal is written or during the proposal stage I'm
brought in [sniffle]—and I get to do the work. (Reproduced
from Tremblay, 1990)

This text is a good example of an interviewer's listening hard to a
participant. At the beginning of the interview, the participant is not quite
focused. The interviewer, concentrating on what he is saying, nudges him
into the frame of reference of the second interview. Once she has the participant in the right channel, she listens and lets him talk. Even when the
participant pauses for a few seconds, she does not interrupt.

Patai (1987) describes the process of listening to her Brazilian women participants as an intense form of concentration and openness to them that led her to become absorbed in them (p. 12). Although not every interview takes on the almost magical quality that Patai describes, interest in the participant's experience and a willingness to hold one's own ego in check are keys to the hard work of listening in an interview that leads to the type of absorption Patai describes.

FOLLOW UP ON WHAT THE PARTICIPANT SAYS

When interviewers do talk in an interview, they usually ask questions. The key to asking questions during in-depth interviewing is to let them follow, as much as possible, from what the participant is saying. Although the interviewer comes to each interview with a basic question that establishes the purpose and focus of the interview, it is in response to what the participant says that the interviewer follows up, asks for clarification, seeks concrete details, and requests stories. While interviewers may develop preset interviewing guides to which they will refer when the timing is right, interviewers' initial basic work in this approach to interviewing is to listen actively and to move the interview forward as much as possible by building on what the participant has begun to share.

Ask Questions When You Do Not Understand

It is hard work to understand everything people say. Sometimes the context is not clear. At other times we do not understand the specific referent of what someone is saying. In everyday conversation we often let such things slide by without understanding them. In interviewing such sliding undermines the process.

The interview structure is cumulative. One interview establishes the context for the next. Not having understood something in an early interview, an interviewer might miss the significance of something a participant says later. Passages in interviews become links to each other in ways that cannot be foretold. Also, the interviewer who lets a participant know when he or she does not understand something shows the person that the interviewer is listening.

Sometimes it is difficult to get the chronology of an experience straight. It is important for interviewers to understand experiences in the context of time. A question like, "Can you tell me again when that happened?" is a reasonable one. I use the word *again* so as not to imply to participants that they are not being clear, thereby making them defensive, but rather, as is often the case, to suggest that I was just not attentive enough the first time around.

Sometimes participants use vague words that seem to be communicating but are not explicit. For example, one community college faculty member whom I interviewed consistently described his students by saying, "They are very nice." I did not know what he meant by the term *nice.* In a way it seemed to trivialize the respect for his students that he had communicated throughout the interview. I asked him, "What is *nice*?" He said,

> The students at the private university [where he had previously taught] were rude, and they were frequently demanding. I don't mean intellectually demanding. They would say, "You didn't say that. You didn't say you were going to test us on that sort of thing." Our students at the community college are really nice. I realize this sounds silly; I apologize for it. It really sounds crazy to say for some reason we happen to have the nicest people around that happen to live in this neighborhood. Now that's not likely. But we have an attitude on this campus. There is a kind of mutual respect and I get a lot of this when our students come back after they have gone somewhere else. . . . There is a different feeling, even though it is a bigger school, and you really don't know everybody. Uh, nonetheless there is a kind of community feeling here and there is a lack of what I call a mean spirit where you are just touchy and aggressive and, uh, inquisitive. Maybe our students are not that motivated; maybe that's why they are not; but they are really nice to teach. You almost never have anything you could call a discipline problem. It just doesn't happen. . . . I don't know; I do like our students. I think it would be absolutely perfect if they were a little better prepared, but that's not as important as being nice people. . . . They are the kind of people that are pleasant to work with. (Interview in Seidman et al., 1983)

In responding to my request for clarification about his use of the word *nice,* the participant went more deeply into the nature of his teaching experience. By my taking his language seriously, he explored what he meant when he used the word *nice.* As the interviewer, I then understood better what, for him, were the complexities implied in his use of the apparently simple word *nice.*

Ask to Hear More About a Subject

When interviewers want to hear more about what a participant is saying, they should trust that instinct. Interviewers should ask questions when they feel unsatisfied with what they have heard. Sometimes they do not think that they have heard the entire story; other times they may think that they are getting generalities and they want to hear the details; or they may just be interested in what the participant is saying and want to hear more. Sometimes when listening, interviewers begin to feel a vague question welling up inside them because they sense there is more to the story. In those instances it is important for them to ask to hear more.

For example, in a study of older women returning to community colleges (Schatzkamer, 1986), one student spoke about her experience in a math course. The last two thirds of the technical math course she was taking was devoted to calculus.

She said, "At that point, I capsized. That was beyond the capacities of my math . . . it was beyond me. So I was obedient. This is something I don't usually do in school, but I just memorized and did what I was told and followed out the formulas the way I was told I should and which I regret. I got an A, but I regret it."

The interviewer, hearing the phrase "I regret it," wanted to hear more. She asked, based on what the participant had said, "What do you regret?"

The participant responded, "I never really understood it, you know. I didn't really learn. I'm sure there is something lovely there under all that calculus to be learned and I didn't learn that. I theoretically learned how to use it as a tool. By being slavish you know: plugging numbers into formulas and finding the right formula and stuff; that's not the way math should be learned and it's not really understanding."

By following up on the participant's phrase of regret, the interviewer gave the participant a chance to go a step further in her story. In so doing she revealed a desire to learn and a potential appreciation for the beauty of math that increases the reader's understanding of her community college experience and our respect for her as an individual.

Explore, Don't Probe

In referring to the skill of following up on what participants say, the literature on interviewing often uses the word *probe*. (See, e.g., Lincoln & Guba, 1985; Rubin & Rubin, 1995.) I have never been comfortable with that word. I always think of a sharp instrument pressing on soft flesh when I hear it. The word also conveys a sense of the powerful interviewer treating the participant as an object. I am more comfortable with the notion of exploring with the participant than with probing into what the participant says.

At the same time, too much and ill-timed exploration of the participant's words can make him or her defensive and shift the meaning making from the participant to the interviewer. The interview can become too easily a vehicle for the interviewer's agenda rather than an exploration of the participant's experience. Too little exploration, however, can leave an interviewer unsure of the participant's meaning in the material he or she has gathered. It can also leave the participant using abstractions and generalities that are not useful (Hyman et al., 1954).

LISTEN MORE, TALK LESS, AND ASK REAL QUESTIONS

Listen more, talk less. I repeat the first principle of interviewing here for emphasis and because it is so easy to forget. When you do ask questions, ask only real questions. By a real question I mean one to which the interviewer does not already know or anticipate the response. If interviewers want to ask a question to which they think they know the response, it would be better to say what they think, and then to ask the participant what he or she thinks of the assertion.

Avoid Leading Questions

A leading question is one that influences the direction the response will take. Sometimes the lead is in the intonation of the question: The tone implies an expectation. Sometimes it is in the wording, syntax, and intonation of the question, as when an interviewer asks, "Did you *really* mean to do that?" Sometimes the lead is in the conclusion implied by the question. One interviewer, listening to a participant's story about her family and her early schooling, asked: "Your parents pushed you to study, didn't they?" Or in another place, the interviewer asked, "How satisfied were you with your student teaching placement?" instead of, for example, "What was your student teaching placement like for you?" (For a more extensive discussion of leading questions, see Kvale, 1996; Patton, 1989; Richardson et al., 1965.)

Ask Open-ended Questions

An open-ended question, unlike a leading question, establishes the territory to be explored while allowing the participant to take any direction he or she wants. It does not presume an answer. There are at least two types of open-ended questions especially relevant to in-depth interviewing. One is what Spradley (1979) calls the "grand tour" question (pp. 86–87), in which the interviewer asks the participant to reconstruct a significant segment of an experience. For example, in interviewing a counselor, an interviewer might say, "Take me through a day in your work life." Or in working with a student teacher, an interviewer might ask, "Reconstruct your day for me from the time you wake up to the time you go to bed."

There is also the mini-tour, in which the interviewer asks the participant to reconstruct the details of a more limited time span or of a particular experience. For example, an interviewer might ask a vice principal to reconstruct the details of a particular disciplinary session with a student; or an interviewer might ask a teacher to talk about the experience of a particular conference with a parent.

A second type of open-ended question focuses more on the subjective experience of the participant than on the external structure. For example, a participant might begin to talk about her experience in a parent conference. After asking her what happened at the conference, the interviewer might ask her to talk about what that conference was like for her.

Although there are many approaches to open-ended questioning, when I am interested in understanding the participant's subjective experience, I often find myself asking the question, "What was that like for you?" As Schutz (1967) indicated, it is not possible to experience what the participant experienced. If we could, then we would be the participant. Perhaps the closest we can come is to ask the metaphorical question implied in the word *like*. When interviewers ask what something was like for participants, they are giving them the chance to reconstruct their experience according to their own sense of what was important, unguided by the interviewer. (For a thoughtful discussion of questioning strategies she uses in oral history interviewing, see Yow, 1994, pp. 38–44.)

FOLLOW UP, BUT DON'T INTERRUPT

Avoid interrupting participants when they are talking. Often an interviewer is more interested in something a participant says than the speaker seems to be. While the participant continues talking, the interviewer feels strongly tempted to interrupt to pursue the interesting point. Rather than doing so, however, the interviewer can jot down the key word and follow up on it later, when doing so will not interrupt the participant's train of thought. The opportunity may come later in the same interview or even in a subsequent one (Richardson et al., 1965).

Once, for example, a teacher had been talking early in the second interview about the frenetic pace of her day and about having no place to hide. At the time, I was very interested in what she said, but she went right on to other aspects of her experience. Rather than interrupting her then, I wrote down in my working notes the phrases "frenetic pace" and "no place to hide."

Later, when there was a pause in her responses, I returned to those phrases by saying, "A while back you talked about a very frenetic pace. You talked about coming in the door, teaching your class, walking to your office, keeping extensive hours, having no place to hide. Would you talk more about that frenetic pace and having no place to hide?" (Richardson et al. [1965, pp. 157–163] term this approach "the echo" and caution against its overuse. Weiss [1994, pp. 77–78], however, says that it is important to return to words and phrases that serve as "markers" of something that may be very important to a participant, but for which you might not want to interrupt at the time.)

The participant responded by talking about the effect of her community college's architecture on her daily life. In order to make faculty as accessible as possible to students, the designers of her campus had made the wall of faculty offices that faced the hallway of glass. The participant spoke about her frustration with never having a place to go in her building where she could get some work done without being seen and, most likely, interrupted. Although she could close the door of her office, she could never close out those who sought her.

TWO FAVORITE APPROACHES

Every interviewer probably develops favorite approaches to participants. I have two to which I return often.

Ask Participants to Talk to You as if You Were Someone Else

I use the first approach when I sense that I am hearing a public voice and I am searching for an inner one (see above). In those situations, I often use what Patton (1989) calls role-playing questions (see also Spradley, 1979). I try to figure out the person with whom the participant might be most comfortable talking personally. I then try asking the participant to imagine that I am that person.

I might say, "If I were your spouse (or your father, or your teacher, or your friend), what would you say to me?" Sometimes this question falls flat. I am unable to shift the participant's frame of reference enough so that he or she talks to me as though I were someone else. But often, if used sparingly, the role-playing approach works. The participant takes on a different voice, becomes animated in a way that he or she has not been until then, and both the participant and I enjoy for a few moments the new roles that we have assumed.

Ask Participants to Tell a Story

I also often ask participants to tell me a story about what they are discussing. In a sense, everything said in an interview is a story. But if a participant were talking about, for example, relationships with students, I might ask for a story about one particular student who stands out in his or her experience.

Not everybody is comfortable with being asked directly to tell a story. The request seems to block people who may think they do not tell good stories or that story telling is something only other people do. Others, however, suddenly remember a particular incident, become deeply engrossed in reconstructing it, and tell a wonderful story that conveys their experience as concretely as anything could.

I will always remember the story one student teacher told when she was describing the trouble she was having figuring out how to relate to her students. She had envisioned herself as a friendly older sister to them. One day she overheard a group of her students telling dirty jokes, and she told them a mild one.

About a week later, the vice principal called her to his office to say that parents were outraged about the joke. The student teacher went on to tell of a series of meetings with parents in which she had to explain herself. She described the vice principal's lack of real support during those meetings. Finally she talked about the sobering realization that she had not known where to draw the line with her students. She said, "The dirty joke was horrendous, and I understood that. I understood that I was just trying to be one of the kids, that I felt close to them. . . . I was just being too familiar. I always thought that teaching . . . was relating to the kids."

Stories such as this, in which the student teacher gave a beginning, middle, and end to a segment of her experience, drew characters, presented conflict, and showed how she dealt with it, convey experience in an illuminating and memorable way. (See Mishler, 1986, chap. 4, for an extended discussion of the power of narratives, and Mattingly, 1998, chaps. 1 and 2 for the complexities of stories and narratives.) If an interviewer continually asks participants to illustrate experiences with a story, the technique will wear out quickly. Used sparingly, however, and targeted at particular aspects of the participant's experience, it can lead to treasured moments in interviewing.

ASK PARTICIPANTS TO RECONSTRUCT, NOT TO REMEMBER

Avoid asking participants to rely on their memories. As soon as interviewers ask if people remember something, impediments to memory spring up (Tagg, 1985). Ask participants, in effect, not to remember their experience but rather to reconstruct it. Ask directly "What happened?" or "What was your elementary school experience like?" instead of "Do you remember what your elementary school experience was like?"

Interviewers can assume that the participants will be able to reconstruct their experience and thereby avoid many of the impediments to memory that abound. Reconstruction is based partially on memory and partially on what the participant now senses is important about the past event. In a sense, all recall is reconstruction (Thelen, 1989). In interviewing, it is better to go for that reconstruction as directly as possible.

KEEP PARTICIPANTS FOCUSED AND
ASK FOR CONCRETE DETAILS

Keep participants focused on the subject of the interview. If they begin to talk about current experience in the first interview, try to guide them back to the focus of that interview, which is to provide contextual background from their life story. Although the interviewer must avoid a power struggle, he or she must offer enough guidance in the process so that participants can come to respect the structure and individual purpose of each of the three interviews in the series.

Throughout the interviews, but especially in the first two, ask for concrete details of a participant's lived experience before exploring attitudes and opinions about it. The concrete details constitute the experience; attitudes and opinions are based on them. Without the concrete details, the attitudes and opinions can seem groundless.

DO NOT TAKE THE EBBS AND FLOWS OF
INTERVIEWING TOO PERSONALLY

Watch for an ebb and flow in interviews and try not to take it too personally. In-depth interviewing often surprises participants because they have seldom had the opportunity to talk at length to someone outside their family or friends about their experience. As a result, they may become so engrossed in the first interview that they say things that they are later surprised they have shared (Spradley, 1979; Kirsch, 1999). Interviewers often arrive at the second interview thinking what a wonderful interview the first was, only to be surprised that now the participants pull back and are not willing to share as much as before. (Young & Lee, 1996, identify a similar phenomenon; see p. 106.) At this point, interviewers have to be careful not to press too hard for the type of sharing they experienced before. The third interview allows participants to find a zone of sharing within which they are comfortable. They resolve the issue for themselves.

LIMIT YOUR OWN INTERACTION

Only Share Experiences Occasionally

There are times when an interviewer's experience may connect to that of the participant. Sharing that experience in a frank and personal way may encourage the participant to continue reconstructing his or her own in a more inner voice than before. Overused, however, such sharing can distort an interview and distract participants from their own experience to the interviewer's. I can remember sharing stories of mine that I thought connected to what the participant was saying and sensing that the participant was impatient for me to stop talking. (For a somewhat different perspective on the amount of interaction that is desirable between interviewer and participant, see Oakley, 1981.)

Avoid Reinforcing Your Participants' Responses

Avoid reinforcing what your participant is saying, either positively or negatively. A useful training exercise is to transcribe verbatim 5 minutes of an early interview. What sometimes becomes clear is that the interviewer is in the habit of saying "uh huh" or "OK" or "yes" or some other short affirmative response to almost every statement from the participant. Sometimes interviewers are hardly aware that they are doing it.

On having such reinforcement called to their attention, many new interviewers suggest that there is nothing inappropriate about the practice. They argue that it shows they are listening and being attentive and that participants appreciate knowing that; it keeps them talking. Often, I think, it is a relatively benign controlling mechanism that is difficult to give up.

But interviewers who reinforce what they are hearing run the risk of distorting how the participant responds. A more effective and less invasive method is to refer later in an interview to something participants said earlier. (For a more balanced perspective on reinforcements, see Richardson et al., 1965.)

EXPLORE LAUGHTER

Often a participant will say something and then laugh, sometimes because what he or she just said is self evidently funny. At other times, the laughter may be nervous or ironic, its origin unclear to the interviewer and often worth exploring. For example, when interviewing a female science teacher, I asked her how the fact that there were 10 women in her community college science division of 60 faculty affected her sense of power in the college. I related the question to Rosabeth Moss Kanter's discussion of numbers and power in her book, *Men and Women of the Corporation* (1977). The participant responded:

> Well, you see this isn't a corporation. I mean, people are not jockeying for position within, and that would make a tremendous difference, I think, if we were really competitive with one another for something, [laugh] it might be a tremendously important factor. But we're not competing for anything. There are very few people who want to, say, go up to the next step, which is division director. I feel I could get elected to division director, if I so chose. [Pause] My sex would not at all interfere. [Pause] It might even be a plus, but, uh, most people here are not interested, it's not a power play situation; we're all retired really [laugh]. (Interview in Seidman et al., 1983)

After she finished and I weighed in my mind the juxtaposition of her laughter with what she was saying, I said, "That sounds bitter." In reply, she spoke about the positive and negative aspects in her experience of not being in a highly competitive, upwardly mobile faculty. I did not follow up at that point because I thought doing so might make her defensive. I wrote in my working notes, "laughter?" and came back to it later in the interview. As Studs Terkel has said, "A laugh can be a cry of pain, and a silence can be a shout" (Parker, 1996, p. 165).

FOLLOW YOUR HUNCHES

Follow your hunches. Trust your instincts. When appropriate, risk saying what you think or asking the difficult question. Sometimes during an interview, a question will start to form, perhaps first as a vague impression, then as a real doubt. My experience is that it is important to trust those responses, to figure out the question that best expresses them, and to ask it.

During one interview with an intern teacher, I became increasingly uncomfortable. I could not figure out what was bothering me until I realized that the participant was talking positively about his teaching experience in a very formal way but with very little energy. His nonverbal language was contradicting his verbal language. I began to think he was really very unhappy with his teaching, even though he was talking relatively positively about it.

I was very uncomfortable with this hunch, but finally after we were more than two thirds of the way into the second interview, I said to him, "You know, I can't figure this out. You are talking as though you are enjoying your teaching, but something about the way you are talking makes me think you are not. Is that fair?"

He responded as though I had opened a floodgate. He began to talk about how angry he was that intern teachers got all the "lowest" classes. He said that even though he had solid math preparation, he would not have a chance to teach upper-level courses for perhaps 5 more years, because all course assignments were made on the basis of seniority. Then he talked about how hard he worked, how little time he had on weekends to be with his wife, and how little money he was making. As a result of following up on a hunch, I gained a completely different picture of his experience, and in the rest of the interview his verbal and nonverbal language coincided.

USE AN INTERVIEW GUIDE CAUTIOUSLY

Some forms of interviewing depend on an interview guide. (See, e.g., Yow, 1994.) The interviewers arrive with preset questions to which they want answers or about which they want to gather data. In-depth interviewing, however, is not designed to test hypotheses, gather answers to questions, or corroborate opinions. Rather, it is designed to ask participants to reconstruct their experience and to explore their meaning. The questions most used in an in-depth interview follow from what the participant has said.

Nonetheless, in-depth interviewers may want to develop an interviewing guide. The basic structure of the interview is the question that establishes the focus of each interview in the series. However, interviewers never come into an interview situation as clean slates. They have interests, or they would not have chosen the research topic they did. In addition, some participants will require more prompting than others to go forward in the reconstruction of their experience. Also, over the course of a number of interviews, the interviewer may notice that several participants have highlighted a particular issue, and the interviewer may want to know how other participants would respond to that issue.

For these reasons, in our study of the experience of student teachers we developed a guide that listed the following areas: student teachers' relationship with mentors, with students, with other student teachers, with parents, with tracking, testing, and grading. In most cases, student teachers raised these topics on their own as they talked about their teaching experience. In those instances when they did not, and if there was an opportunity to do so without interrupting or diverting a participant's reconstruction of his or her own experience, the interviewer referred to the interview guide and raised an issue that had not been touched upon.

If interviewers decide to use an interview guide, they must avoid manipulating their participants to respond to it. Interviewers should ask questions that reflect areas of interest to them in an open and direct way, perhaps acknowledging that the question comes more from their own interest than from what the participant has said. Interviewers must try to avoid imposing their own interests on the experience of the participants. Interviewers working with an interview guide must allow for the possibility that what may interest them or other participants may be of little interest to the person being interviewed. Interview guides can be useful but must be used with caution. (For the development of interview guides, see Weiss, 1994, pp. 45–51.)

TOLERATE SILENCE

Interviewers sometimes get impatient and uncomfortable with silence. They project that discomfort onto their participants. They see pauses as voids and jump into the interview with a quick question to fill the void. A useful exercise is to play back an interview tape and record how much time the interviewer gives the participant to think before he or she jumps in with a question. My experience is that new interviewers think they are waiting a considerable time before asking their next question, but when we go over audiotapes of their interviews, we determine that in reality they are waiting only a second or two. Thoughtfulness takes time; if interviewers can learn to tolerate either the silence that sometimes follows a question or a pause within a participant's reconstruction, they may hear things they would never have heard if they had leapt in with another question to break the silence. (See Mary-Budd Rowe, 1974, on the effect of how much time teachers wait for answers to questions on the quality of students' responses.)

On the other hand, Yow (1994, p. 63) and Gordon (1987) point out that too long a studied silence on the part of the interviewer can put undue pressure on the participant. The interviewer's staying silent too long can turn a "pregnant or permissive pause" into an "embarrassing silence" (Gordon, 1987, pp. 423, 426).

As in other aspects of interviewing, there is a delicate balance between jumping in too soon with a question and waiting too long in silence. There are no rules of thumb here. It is important to give your participant space to think, reflect, and add to what he or she has said. This may take a second or two for some participants and 20 seconds for others.

CONCLUSION

There is no recipe for the effective question. The truly effective question flows from an interviewer's concentrated listening, engaged interest in what is being said, and purpose in moving forward. Sometimes an important question will start out as an ill-defined instinct or hunch, which takes time to develop and seems risky to ask. Sometimes the effective question reflects the interviewer's own groping for coherence about what is being said and is asked in a hesitant, unsure manner.

Effective questioning is so context-bound, such a reflection of the relationship that has developed between the interviewer and the participant, that to define it further runs the risk of making a human process mechanical. To some extent, the way interviewers are as people will be the way they are as interviewers. If interviewers are the sort of people who always have to be talking, who never listen, who demand to be the center of attention most of the time, who are really not interested in other people's stories, no matter what procedures they follow in interviewing, those characteristics will probably pervade the interviewing relationship.

The most important personal characteristic interviewers must have is a genuine interest in other people. They must be deeply aware that other people's stories are of worth in and of themselves as well as for the usefulness of what they offer to interviewers' research. With a temperament that finds interest in others, a person has the foundation upon which to learn the techniques of interviewing and to practice its skills.

Chapter 7

Interviewing as a Relationship

Interviewing is both a research methodology and a social relationship that must be nurtured, sustained, and then ended gracefully (Dexter, 1970; Hyman et al., 1954; Mishler, 1986). In part, each interviewing relationship is individually crafted. It is a reflection of the personalities of the participant and the interviewer and the ways they interact. The relationship is also a reflection of the purpose, structure, and method of in-depth interviewing. For example, the fact that the participant and the interviewer meet three times over 2 or 3 weeks results in a relationship different from that which would result from a single-interview structure.

Interviewers can try to craft relationships with their participants that are like islands of interchange separate from the world's definitions, classifications, and tensions. However, individual interviewing relationships exist in a social context. Although an interviewer might attempt to isolate the interviewing relationship from that context and make it unique to the interviewer and the participant, the social forces of class, ethnicity, race, and gender, as well as other social identities, impose themselves. Although interviewers may try to ignore these social forces, they tend to affect their relationships with participants nonetheless.

INTERVIEWING AS AN "I–THOU" RELATIONSHIP

In a section of his book that is elegant even in translation, Schutz (1967) explains that one person's intersubjective understanding of another depends upon creating an "I–Thou" relationship, a concept bearing both similarities to and significant differences from the philosopher Martin Buber's use of the phrase. "Thou" is someone close to the interviewer, still separate, but a fellow person. We recognize "Thou," according to Schutz, as another "alive and conscious human being" (p. 164). Implicit in such an "I–Thou" relationship is a shift from the interviewer's seeing the participant as an object or a type, which he or she would normally describe syntactically in the third person. Schutz goes on to say that a relationship in which each person is "Thou" oriented—that is, in which the sense of "Thou-ness" is mutual—becomes a "We" relationship.

The interviewer's goal is to transform his or her relationship with the participant into an "I–Thou" relationship that verges on a "We" relationship. In the approach to interviewing I have been discussing, the interviewer does not strive for a full "We" relationship. In such a case the interviewer would become an equal participant, and the resulting discourse would be a conversation, not an interview. In an "I–Thou" relationship, however, the interviewer keeps enough distance to allow the participant to fashion his or her responses as independently as possible.

In some approaches to participatory research, however, the interviewers do attempt to create a full "We" relationship (Griffin, 1989; Reason, 1994). Oakley (1981) argues that not doing so is manipulative and reflects a male, hierarchical model of research. (See de Laine, 2000, pp. 108–116; Stacey, 1988, for respectful but critical discussions of the feminist position Oakley's perspective represents.) I try to strike a balance, saying enough about myself to be alive and responsive but little enough to preserve the autonomy of the participant's words and to keep the focus of attention on his or her experience rather than mine.

RAPPORT

That balancing act is central to developing an appropriate rapport with the participant. I have never been completely comfortable with the common assumption that the more rapport the interviewer can establish with the participant, the better. Rapport implies getting along with each other, a harmony with, a conformity to, an affinity for one another. The problem is that, carried to an extreme, the desire to build rapport with the participant can transform the interviewing relationship into a full "We" relationship in which the question of whose experience is being related and whose meaning is being made is critically confounded.

In our community college study, one participant invited my wife and me to his house for dinner after the second interview and before the third. I had never had such an invitation from a participant in the study, and I did not quite know what to do. I did not want to appear ungracious, so we accepted. My wife and I went to dinner at his home. We had a wonderful California backyard cookout, and it was a pleasure to spend time with the participant and his family. But a few days later, when I met him at his faculty office for the third interview, he was so warm and familiar toward me that I could not retain the distance I needed to explore his responses. I felt tentative as an interviewer because I did not want to risk violating the spirit of hospitality that he had created by inviting us to his home.

The rapport an interviewer must build in an interviewing relationship needs to be controlled. Too much or too little rapport can lead to distortion of what the participant reconstructs in the interview (Hyman et al., 1954). For the sake of establishing rapport, for example, interviewers sometimes share their own experience when they think it is relevant to the participant's. Although such sharing may contribute to building rapport, it can also affect and even distort what the participant might have said had the interviewer not shared his or her experience. The interviewing relationship must be marked by respect, interest, attention, and good manners on the part of the interviewer. The interviewer must be constantly alert to what is appropriate to the situation. As in teaching, the interviewing relationship can be friendly but not a friendship. On this subject, Judy Stacey (1988, p. 24) is especially compelling. She warns that the greater the intimacy and the apparent mutuality of the relationship between the researcher and the researched, the greater is the danger of the exploitation of the participant.

At the beginning of an interviewing relationship, I recommend erring on the side of formality rather than familiarity. (See also Hyman et al., 1954.) For example, an early step in an interviewing relationship is to ask if the participant minds being called by his or her first name. To do so without asking presumes familiarity, which can be off-putting, especially to older people. Common courtesies such as holding a door, not sitting until the person is seated, and introducing yourself again so that you make sure the participant knows to whom he or she is talking are small steps. But they all add up to expressing respect for the participant, which is central to the interview process.

Once the interview is under way, and as the participant begins to share his or her life history and details of present experience, it is crucial for the interviewer to maintain a delicate balance between respecting what the participant is saying and taking advantage of opportunities to ask difficult questions, to go more deeply into controversial subjects. In our seminar on In-Depth Interviewing and Issues in Qualitative Research, for example, one interviewer said that a participant had made remarks that reflected what the interviewer thought to be racist attitudes. At the time, which was early in her pilot project, the interviewer did not feel comfortable in following up on that aspect of what the participant had said. She hadn't yet developed a technique for exploring such a difficult subject without appearing judgmental. However, by not following up, she later realized that she was left with material which, if used, might be unfair to the participant. She decided that she could not use the material. (See de Laine, 2000, pp. 197–203; Lee, 1993, pp. 187–194, for discussions of self-censorship that researchers sometimes impose on themselves.) In future interviews she would find a tactful way to encourage her participants to explore their own words further when she perceived ambiguity in their narrative.

Another reason to control the rapport an interviewer builds in an interviewing relationship is that when the interviews are concluded, the interviewing relationship shifts dramatically. It becomes more distant, less intimate, focusing on what happens to the material generated by the interview. Issues of ownership of the material can easily arise. Interviewers should agree to give a copy of the transcripts or audiotapes to the participant, who has a basic right to these. The participant may want to review the transcripts to see if there is any part with which he or she might not be comfortable and wish to have excluded from the study. This stage of the relationship is likely to be conducted by phone, letter, or e-mail. The rapport an interviewer builds during the interview must be consistent with the relationship the interviewer expects to have with the participant after the interviews are concluded. (See Griffin, 1989, for a model of an active, ongoing relationship between interviewers and participants.)

Once the interviewer writes a report on the interviews, he or she may share the report with the participants. Lincoln and Guba (1985) refer to such sharing as member-checking, and they indicate that it contributes to the trustworthiness and credibility of the report. But difficult issues can arise at this point. Some interviewers give a right of review to the participant that can amount almost to a veto on how the interviewer works with, analyzes, and writes up the results of the interviewing project. Some researchers go further and suggest that the participant in the interview should also become a participant in working with the material (Griffin, 1989). The stances researchers take on this issue are wide ranging (Patai, 1987). At one end of the continuum are those who argue for a type of co-ownership. At the other are those who suggest that the relationship ends with the interview, and the only obligations that the writer has are to make sure the participants knew why they were being interviewed and the interviewer has not distorted the spirit of what the participant said.

My practice has been to offer to share with participants any material that concerns them. I especially want to know if in working with the interview data I have done anything that makes them vulnerable, or if I have presented anything that is not accurate. Except with regard to issues of vulnerability or inaccuracy, however, I retain the right to write the final report as I see it. At the same time, I would hold myself to the principle de Laine (2000, p. 191) articulates: not saying anything in print that I would not say directly to my participants. (In her study of high schools, Lightfoot, 1983, tells of the awkward situation she encountered when participants in her study disagreed with her interpretations.)

The type of relationship the interviewer anticipates after the interview is concluded affects the nature of the relationship the interviewer nurtures during it. If the interviewer has created a full "We" relationship in the process of the interviewing, then he or she must be prepared to deal with the consequences when the time comes to work with the material generated in an interview and report on it. To establish such a deeply sharing, mutually intimate interviewing relationship and then claim one-sided ownership of the material at the conclusion of the interview may cause problems. On the other hand, an interviewer who is explicit about the rights of the participant before the interview begins, and who controls the distance he or she keeps with the participant, establishes the condition for an equitable relationship when working with the material.

SOCIAL GROUP IDENTITIES AND
THE INTERVIEWING RELATIONSHIP

Issues of equity in an interviewing relationship are affected by the social identities that participants and interviewers bring to the interview. Our social identities are affected by our experience with issues of class, race, ethnicity, and gender, and those social forces interact with the sense of power in our lives (Kanter, 1977). The interviewing relationship is fraught with issues of power—who controls the direction of the interview, who controls the results, who benefits. To negotiate these variables in developing an equitable interviewing relationship, the interviewer must be acutely aware of his or her own experience with them as well as sensitive to the way these issues may be affecting the participants.

Race and Ethnicity

In our society, with its history of racism, researchers and participants of different racial and ethnic backgrounds face difficulties in establishing an effective interviewing relationship. It is especially complex for Whites and African Americans to interview each other, but other interracial or cross-ethnic pairings can also be problematic. (To explore this important issue more deeply, see Boushel, 2000; Dexter, 1970; Dollard, 1949; Hyman et al., 1954; Labov, 1972; Phoenix, 1994; Reese, Danielson, Shoemaker, Chang, & Hsu, 1986; Richardson et al., 1965; Song & Parker, 1995.) In addition, interviewing relationships between those of the same racial-ethnic background but of different gender, class, and age can engender tensions that inhibit the full development of an effective interviewing relationship.

That is not to say that individual interviewers and participants cannot to some extent subvert the societal context in which we do our research. Interviewers and participants of good will who are from different racial backgrounds can create a relationship that runs counter to prevailing social currents. Maintaining sensitivity to issues that trigger distrust as well as exhibiting good manners, respect, and a genuine interest in the stories of others can go a long way toward bridging racial and ethnic barriers.

Such bridging attempts are methodologically important. Although the shared assumptions that come from common backgrounds may make it easier to build rapport, interviewing requires interviewers to have enough distance to enable them to ask real questions and to explore, not to share, assumptions. It would be an unfortunate methodological situation if African Americans could interview only other African Americans, Latinos only other Latinos, Asian Americans only other Asian Americans, Native Americans only other Native Americans, and Whites only other Whites.

In my own experience, I have found that the three-interview structure goes some way toward overcoming the initial distrust that can be present when a White person interviews an African American. The three-interview structure can mitigate tensions in other cross-racial interviewing relationships as well. By returning to the participant three times, an interviewer has the opportunity to demonstrate respect, thoughtfulness, and interest in that individual, all of which can work toward ameliorating skepticism. Nonetheless, my experience is that racial politics can make interracial and cross-ethnic interviewing, no matter the structure of the interviews and the sensitivity of the interviewers, difficult to negotiate.

Of the 76 faculty and administrative participants we interviewed in our community college study (Seidman et al., 1983), only one terminated the interviews before the series was completed. That participant was a male, African American administrator at a community college who withdrew near the end of the first interview. At the time, he gave no reason. He just said that he wanted to stop.

I remember the feeling of disappointment as my colleague Sullivan and I left the interview. We searched our minds for what had precipitated his decision. I felt both guilty and disheartened and was on the verge of losing confidence in the interviewing methodology. Later, as I reflected further on the episode, I realized that our interview study had become caught up in the racial history and politics of our society. Perhaps instead of being a failure, our interview method had been working too well. As our participant had spoken of his life history, he had begun to deal with the way racism had played out in his life and his career. I think he found himself speaking more honestly to White interviewers than he cared to (Anderson, Silver, & Abramson, 1988; Cotter, Cohen, & Coulter, 1982). His withdrawing was a loss to us and our study.

Linda Miller Cleary met a similarly complex situation in her research on American Indian education. Cleary prepares teachers of secondary English at the University of Minnesota, Duluth. She has a significant number of students who are Ojibwe, and most will teach American Indian students. She developed a research project, initially to find out more about the experience of teachers of American Indian students to better prepare her students to do that work. In an interview with me in 1996, Cleary said that she felt "always suspect" whenever she sought access to American Indian educators. She said she sensed a distrust of her motives and intentions. After one series of interviews was completed, one participant asked her pointedly, "Why are you doing this?"

She was well into her research when, because of the suspicion she had faced in establishing access and in each initial interview, she realized that "people aren't going to trust me as an author." Although she felt she had been able to get beyond much of the initial distrust and gather good material in her interviews, she wanted "another perspective . . . in the process of analysis." She came to the decision that, "I really couldn't do it alone . . . the gap was too big" (L. M. Cleary, personal communication, August 11, 1996).

Facing the issue head on, Cleary solved it by inviting a colleague, Thomas Peacock, who holds the Endowed Chair of American Indian Education at her university, to join her in the research project. By teaming with a colleague who knew firsthand the complexities of their American Indian participants' experience, she took a significant step toward strengthening the equity between researchers and participants and the authority of the research. Their collaborative work is represented in their book, *Collected Wisdom: American Indian Education* (Cleary & Peacock, 1997), in which they discuss not only the subject of the research but also the significant methodological issues inherent in it.

Gender

There is evidence that interviewers and participants of different genders get different interviewing results than do those of the same gender (Hyman et al., 1954). The interviewing relationship that develops when participant and interviewer are different genders can be deeply affected by sexist attitudes and behaviors. All the problems that one can associate with sexist gender relationships can be played out in an interview. Males interviewing female participants can be overbearing. Women interviewing men can sometimes be reluctant to control the focus of the interview. Male participants can be too easily dismissive of female interviewers. Interviewers of both genders can fail to see the possibilities of whole areas of exploration if their perspectives are ideologically laden. Nor are interviews among interviewers and participants of the same gender automatically unproblematic. They can be imbued by the false assumption of shared perspectives or a sense of competition never stated.

In addition to affecting individual relationships between interviewers and participants, sexism influences the total context of research. Interviewing research itself can be characterized as "soft" research—research not likely to yield "hard" data—and can thereby be minimized by a sexist research community (Callaway, 1981). On another level, Patai (1987) argues that if interviewers use women for their own research ends, no matter how well-intentioned the research study is, the dominant paradigm of a society's exploiting women is supported rather than challenged.

There is also the possibility of sexual exploitation in in-depth interviewing because of the sense of intimacy that can develop. Participants talk about the details of their lives while the interviewer listens attentively. A natural bond of fondness and respect develops as the interviewer and the participant explore the participant's experience. Clearly, it is important for interviewers not to exploit that bond sexually.

In one study, a research assistant told me how she had become attracted to one of her participants as a result of interviewing. She wanted to talk about her feelings and their implications for the interview process. She knew that any connection with the participant outside the interview structure would serve only to distort the interviewing relationship. She was worried that even if she had no outside contact with the participant, her fond feelings were affecting the way she asked questions. (See Hyman et al., 1954, p. 54, for another example of how the cordiality of the interviewing relationship affects the way interviewers ask questions.) It helped when I assured her that her feelings were reasonable, but I also emphasized the importance of staying focused on the purpose of the interviews.

It is possible for male and female interviewers and participants to subvert the gender-role stereotypes sexist society would have them play. Interviewers of both sexes can study transcripts of interviews they have done, reconstructing the arrangements they have made to see how they might have employed sexist assumptions in building their interviewing relationships. They can also examine those relationships by reflecting on their interviewing experience in a journal or with a peer. Most important, in the interviewing relationship itself, they can demonstrate a consciousness of sexism and concern for gender equity. (For further reading on the subject of gender and interviewing, see an excellent discussion in chapter 5 of Yow, 1994, and an extensive and considered discussion in Devault, 1990. See also Edwards, 1990; Herod, 1993; Riessman, 1987; Rosser, 1992; Williams & Heikes, 1993.)

Class, Hierarchy, and Status

When interviewer and participant eye each other through the lens of class consciousness, the stories told and the experiences shared can be distorted (Hyman et al., 1954). A lack of consciousness about class issues can be injurious to both the participant and the interviewer (Sennett & Cobb, 1972).

In a discussion of class in Marxist terms, Patai (1987) described the interviewer as a hybrid of a capitalist and a laborer who is capable of treating the words of participants as commodities to be exploited. If one understands class as a function of status, education, and wealth, interviewers are often middle class and university based, interviewing those who are in some way lower on a scale of status. (Dexter, 1970, runs counter to that notion.)

When we did our study of community college faculty, I became conscious of their sensitivity to the higher education totem pole. In the context of the university, school of education faculty rank low. Some community college faculty participants, however, treated me with either an unwarranted skepticism because of my affiliation with what they perceived as the ivory tower, or an unearned deference because of my affiliation with a university, in contrast to their self-description of being "just" in a community college.

Even the use of interviewing itself can be affected by class-based assumptions. For example, Richardson et al. (1965) wrote that participants of

> low intelligence, low socio-economic status, or low status in an organized hierarchy may find it difficult to tolerate a preponderance of open questions because they are unused to talking at length spontaneously, articulately, or coherently, or because they are uncomfortable in an unstructured situation. (p. 149).

My experience has been that when participants, whatever their class background, place their work in the context of their life histories and are given the space to tell their stories, they can respond to open-ended questions. On the other hand, when class, gender, or racial tension pervades the interviewing relationship, participants are likely to be tight-lipped and restricted in their responses (Labov, 1972; Patton, 1989).

Some interviewers have a wider range of class versatility than others. Given their own life histories, they are able to operate comfortably with people lower and higher in the class structure than they are. Others' life experience has been so homogeneous that they are comfortable only when they are interviewing participants whose social-class experiences are similar to their own. They are reluctant to interview in settings in which they have little experience or classes of people with whom they have had little contact. That reluctance can sometimes result in a skewed sample of participants being interviewed and a picture of the experience being studied that is narrower than warranted.

Linguistic Differences

An issue embedded in many of the social relationships described above is linguistic differences between interviewers and participants. Sometimes English-speaking researchers interview participants for whom English is not the first language. If interviewers are fluent in the participants' mother tongue and interview in that language, they will subsequently face the complexity of translation. The issue of finding the right word in English or any other language to represent the full sense of the word the participants spoke in their native language is demanding and requires a great deal of care (Vygotsky, 1987).

Some doctoral students with whom I have worked who are fluent in the native language of their participants have experimented with interviewing in English and going along with their participants as they may switch back and forth between English and their mother tongue. When reporting on the interviews, especially in crucial segments, the researchers sometimes report the language of the participants as spoken in the mother tongue to honor that language and the thought patterns inherent in it. They then provide a translation immediately following the portion spoken in the mother tongue.

What is at issue in interviewing participants whose first language is not that of the interviewer is the extent to which the language used by both the participants and the interviewer affects the progress of the interview. The thinking of both the participants and the interviewer is intertwined with the language they are using (Vygotsky, 1987). As in most issues regarding interviewing, there is not one right way to respond to these situations, except to recognize the importance of language and culture to thought. With that awareness, both interviewer and participants can experiment with ways of talking to each other that most authentically reflect their thinking. (For further reading on this subject, see Goldstein, 1995.)

Age

In addition to race, gender, and class, the relative ages of the participant and the interviewer may affect the type of relationship that develops between them. Some older participants may feel uncomfortable being interviewed by a young interviewer, especially if they feel that the interviewer places them in a subordinate role (Briggs, 1986). Interviewing participants who are much younger or much older takes a special type of sensitivity on the part of the interviewer. He or she must know how to connect to children or seniors without patronizing them. When class, race, linguistic, and age differences are combined, especially in groups of school-age children, the danger that an interviewer will elicit distorted responses is high (Brenner et al., 1985). But when interviewed skillfully and with consciousness of class, race, and age, children can be thoughtful about their experience in and out of school and are capable of reflection that is informative and compelling (Labov, 1972). (For an example of effective interviewing of young adults, see Cleary, 1990, 1991.)

Elites

Of the imbalances that can occur in the relationship between interviewer and participant, one of the most difficult to negotiate occurs when researchers try to use an in-depth interviewing approach with people in positions of power. Sally Lynne Conkright (1997) used the method described in this book to interview 11 chief executive officers or those on the next rung of authority in 11 significant U.S. corporations. She met the expected problems of access, which she overcame to a considerable extent. She also faced serious problems in carrying out her interviewing plan. Executives who had agreed in advance to 90-minute interviews would develop very busy schedules. By the time she arrived for the interview, some could or would only give her a shorter amount of time.

On a different level, she noted that elites are often accustomed to being in charge of situations in which they find themselves. A number of her participants tried to take charge of the interviews. Sometimes, when Conkright tried to direct the interview, she noted that her participants became uncomfortable. "In some instances," she wrote, "the signals were nonverbal in nature and, in other instances, the participants verbally expressed that they would direct the interview" (pp. 274–275). She had to walk a very narrow line between asking questions in which she was interested and recognizing that such questions might threaten to lead to the termination of the interview.

Despite these complexities, she sustained her research and learned a great deal about both her subject and the methodology as applied to interviewing elites. Although I see in-depth interviewing as most appropriate for getting at the details of everyday experience of those in less power-laden and status-oriented positions, still the attempt to gain the inner perspective of elites is worthwhile and important. (For further reading on this topic, see Dexter, 1970; Hertz & Imber, 1995.)

DISTINGUISH AMONG PRIVATE, PERSONAL, AND PUBLIC EXPERIENCES

Interviewing relationships are also shaped by what the interviewer and participant deem are appropriate subjects to explore in the interview. In considering what is appropriate, interviewers may find it useful to distinguish among public, personal, and private aspects of a participant's life (Shils, 1959). The public aspect is what participants do, for example, at work or at school, in meetings, in classes, in offices where their actions are subject to the scrutiny of others. Interviewers tend to be most comfortable exploring these public aspects of participants' experience.

Participants' private lives involve matters of intimacy, like aspects of relationships participants do not discuss with outsiders for fear of violating those relationships. Each participant or interviewer may have different boundaries for what he or she considers public, personal, and private. In one interview, I asked a participant to talk more about her engagement, which she had mentioned briefly earlier. She said to me very directly, "That's none of your business."

Participants also have personal lives that bridge their public and private experiences. Personal lives are of at least two basic types. The first is participants' subjective experience of public events. Interviewers tend to feel comfortable exploring that aspect of personal experience. Indeed, that is one of the major functions of interviewing as a research method. The second is participants' experience of events that do not occur in their public lives but in their experience with friends and family away from the workplace or school.

New interviewers tend to be less comfortable exploring experiences in this realm. They often question its relevance to the subject of their study. The dichotomy between what is personal and what is public, however, is often false. What happens in people's personal lives often affects what happens in or provides a context for their public lives and can be useful if tactfully explored in interviewing research. "May I ask," not just as a pro forma statement but seriously meant, is a preface I often put to questions when entering troubling or sensitive areas.

Sometimes interviewers shy away from exploring areas such as death and illness because they themselves are personally uncomfortable, and they assume the participant is too. (See Young & Lee, 1996, for an exploration of the interaction of the feelings of the interviewer with the interview process. Also see Hyman et al., 1954; Rowan, 1981.) If a participant mentions topics such as these, however, he or she thinks they are relevant. To ignore them or not to explore how they might relate to the subject of the research may signal to the participant that what is most important to him or her is somehow not important to the interviewer. If the participant has risked mentioning a personal topic, my experience is that it is important to acknowledge it and to explore the relationship between that personal experience and the subject of the inquiry.

AVOID A THERAPEUTIC RELATIONSHIP

At the same time, interviewers must avoid changing the interviewing relationship into a therapeutic one. Many see a similarity between the type of open-ended, relatively nondirective interviewing that I have been discussing in this book and the type of exploration that takes place in psychotherapy. It is essential that research interviewers not see themselves as therapists. The goals are different (de Laine, 2000, pp. 116–118; Kahn & Cannell, 1960; Kvale, 1996, pp. 155–157; Weiss, 1994, pp. 134–136). The researcher is there to learn, not to treat the participant. The participant did not seek out the researcher and is not a patient. The researcher will see the participant three times, after which their connection will substantially end. They will not have a continuing relationship in which the researcher takes some measure of ongoing responsibility. Researchers are unlikely to be trained therapists. They should know both their own limits and those imposed by the structure and goal of the interviewing process. Researchers must be very cautious about approaching areas of participants' private lives and personal complexities to which they are ill equipped to respond and for which they can take no effective responsibility.

But even when researchers exercise such caution, the intimacy that can develop in in-depth interviewing sometimes threatens those limits, and a participant may find the interviewing process emotionally troubling (Griffin, 1989). Participants may start to cry in an interview. Interviewers may themselves become upset in the face of a participant's tears and not know what to do. My experience is that many times the best thing to do is nothing. (See Brannen, 1988, pp. 559–560, on the importance of listening hard and saying little at times like this in interviews.) Let the participant work out the distress without interfering and taking inappropriate responsibility for it. On the other hand, if the distress continues, the interviewer then has the responsibility to pull back from whatever is causing it. (See Bernard, 1994, p. 220; Smith, 1992, p. 102; Weiss, 1994, pp. 127–131, for further guidance on interviewers' responsibility for their participants.)

In my mind, a key to negotiating potentially troubled waters is to assess how much responsibility the interviewer can effectively take in navigating them. In one interview, a participant referred repeatedly to a colleague's nervous breakdown. As much as I was interested in the subject, I did not follow up on it because the participant's repeated references to it troubled me. We were near the end of the third interview. I was not planning to return to the participant's campus the next week. I would not be able to follow up if exploring the topic caused the participant emotional distress. One boundary I learned to observe was the one that marked where I could take effective responsibility for follow-up and where I could not.

RECIPROCITY

The issue of reciprocity in the interviewing relationship can be troubling. The more the interviewing relationship is charged with issues of race, ethnicity, class, and gender, the more complicated the problem of reciprocity can be. Patai (1987) in her study of Brazilian women, most of whom were poor, agonized over what could be perceived as inequity in her research. She wrote a book (Patai, 1988) based on her findings and gained the benefits that usually accrue from such publication. On the other hand, she felt her participants gained little tangible benefit from their cooperation with her. Rowan (1981) talks about the lack of reciprocity that can lead to alienation in research. He sees it as alienation because the researcher is separating participants from their words and then using those words to his or her own ends.

This is the most problematic aspect of interviewing to me. I am sympathetic to the argument that the researcher gets more out of the process than the participant. I know, however, and others write about (Patai, 1987; Yow, 1994) the type of listening the interviewer brings to the interview. It takes the participants seriously, values what they say, and honors the details of their lives. The reciprocity I can offer in an interview is that which flows from my interest in participants' experience, my attending to what they say, and my honoring their words when I present their experience to a larger public. Although at the conclusion of the interview I do present my participants with a small gift, that gift is only a token of my appreciation in the fullest sense of the word *token*. I use it to say thank you and to mark the conclusion of that part of our interviewing relationship. (See Marshall & Rossman, 1989; Yow, 1994, for a fuller discussion.)

EQUITY

Interviewers and participants are never equal. We can strive to reduce hierarchical arrangements, but usually the participant and the interviewer want and get different things out of the interview. Despite different purposes, researchers can still strive for equity in the process. By equity I mean a balance between means and ends, between what is sought and what is given, between process and product, and a sense of fairness and justice that pervades the relationship between participant and interviewer.

Building equity in the interviewing relationship starts when the interviewer first makes contact with the participant. Equity means the interviewer's going out of his or her way to get the stories of people whose stories are not usually heard. It means the interviewer's not promising what cannot be delivered, and making sure to deliver what is promised. It means being explicit about the purposes and processes of the research. Equity is supported in an explicit written consent form that outlines the rights and responsibilities of the interviewer and the participant in as detailed a manner as reasonable. Equity is involved in scheduling time and place of interviews. Interviewers ask a great deal of participants. It keeps the process fair when interviewers set up times and places that are convenient to the participant and reasonable for the interviewer. Equity is also involved in the technique of interviewing. An interviewer who is intrusive, who constantly reinforces responses he or she may like—who is really looking for corroboration of personal views rather than the story of the participant's experience—is not being fair to the purpose of in-depth interviewing. Being equitable in interviewing research means, as we see in Chapter 8, valuing the words of the participant because those words are deeply connected to that participant's sense of worth. Being equitable in interviewing research means infusing a research methodology with respect for the dignity of those interviewed.

Researchers cannot be expected to resolve all the inequities of society reproduced in their interviewing relationships, but they do have the responsibility to be conscious of them. Some would argue, though, that research in the social sciences that does not confront these problems contributes to them. (See Fay, 1987, for a review of critical research.) My own sense of the matter is that although it is difficult to do equitable research in an inequitable society, equity must be the goal of every in-depth interviewing researcher. Striving for equity is not only an ethical imperative; it is also a methodological one. An equitable process is the foundation for the trust necessary for participants to be willing to share their experience with an interviewer.

Every step of the interview process can be designed and carried out with the idea of equity in mind. But try as one may to be equitable in interviewing research, equity in interviewing is affected by factors such as racism, classism, and sexism originating outside the individual interviewing relationship or taking place within it. What I have come to grasp over the years I have been doing interviewing research is that the equity of an interviewing relationship, and thereby the quality of the interview, is affected and sometimes seriously limited by social inequities. At the same time, individuals committed to equity in research can find a way to become conscious of the issues and their own role in them. They can then devise methods that attempt to subvert those societal constraints. In the process they may end up being able to tell their participants' stories in a way that can promote equity.

Chapter 8

Analyzing, Interpreting, and Sharing Interview Material

R esearch based on in-depth interviewing is labor intensive. There is no substitute for studying the interviews and winnowing the almost 1 million words a study involving 25 participants might yield. (Each series of three interviews can result in 150 double-spaced pages of transcript.) In planning such a study, allow at least as much time for working with the material as for all the steps involved in conceptualizing the study, writing the proposal, establishing access, making contact, selecting participants, and doing the actual interviews.

MANAGING THE DATA

To work with the material that interviewing generates, the researcher first has to make it accessible by organizing it. Keeping track of participants through the participant information forms, making sure the written consent forms are copied and filed in a safe place, labeling audiotapes of interviews accurately, managing the extensive files that develop in the course of working with the transcripts of interviews, and keeping track of decision points in the entire process all require attention to detail, a concern for security, and a system for keeping material accessible. One goal of this administrative work is to be able to trace interview data to the original source on the interview tape at all stages of the research. Another is to be able to contact a participant readily. The simple act of misfiling a written consent form from a participant upon whose material a researcher wants to rely heavily can create hours of extra work and unnecessary anxiety.

The best description I have seen of file management for a qualitative research study is in Lofland (1971). Although there is no one right way to organize the research process and the materials it generates, every moment the researcher spends paying attention to order, labels, filing, and documentation at the beginning and in the formative stages of the study can save hours of frustration later.

KEEPING INTERVIEWING AND ANALYSIS SEPARATE: WHAT TO DO BETWEEN INTERVIEWS

It is difficult to separate the processes of gathering and analyzing data. Even before the actual interviews begin, the researcher may anticipate results on the basis of his or her reading and preparation for the study. Once the interviews commence, the researcher cannot help but work with the material as it comes in. During the interview the researcher is processing what the participant is saying in order to keep the interview moving forward. Afterward, the researcher mentally reviews each interview in anticipation of the next one. If the interviewer is working as part of a research team, the team may get together to discuss what they are learning from the process of the interviews.

Some researchers urge that the two stages be integrated so that each informs the other. (See, e.g., Lincoln & Guba, 1985; Maxwell, 1996; Miles & Huberman, 1984.) They would have interviewers conduct a number of interviews, study and analyze them, frame new questions as a result of what they have found, and then conduct further interviews.

Although the pure separation of generating from analyzing data is impossible, my own approach is to avoid any in-depth analysis of the interview data until I have completed all the interviews. Even though I sometimes identify possibly salient topics in early interviews, I want to do my best to avoid imposing meaning from one participant's interviews on the next. Therefore, I first complete all the interviews. Then I study all the transcripts. In that way I try to minimize imposing on the generative process of the interviews what I think I have learned from other participants.

However, I do not mean to suggest that between interviews, interviewers avoid considering what they have just heard in order not to contaminate the next interview. In fact, I live with the interviews, constantly running them over in my mind and thinking about the next. Others may want to be even more explicit. For example, one doctoral candidate with whom I work explained:

> After listening to and transcribing the interview, I made a list of the follow-up questions I hoped would be included in the next

interview. . . . Having gone over the tape prior to the session, it was fresh in my mind and I was able to reassess the type of information I was getting and write questions to guide me in the next session. (L. Mestre, personal communication, May 7, 1996)

TAPE-RECORDING INTERVIEWS

I have no doubt that in-depth interviews should be tape-recorded; however, the literature reflects varying opinions on this point (Bogdan & Taylor, 1975; Briggs, 1986; Hyman et al., 1954; Lincoln & Guba, 1985; Patton, 1989; Weiss, 1994). I believe that to work most reliably with the words of participants, the researcher has to transform those spoken words into a written text to study. The primary method of creating text from interviews is to tape-record the interviews and to transcribe them. Each word a participant speaks reflects his or her consciousness (Vygotsky, 1987). The participants' thoughts become embodied in their words. To substitute the researcher's paraphrasing or summaries of what the participants say for their actual words is to substitute the researcher's consciousness for that of the participant. Although inevitably the researcher's consciousness will play a major role in the interpretation of interview data, that consciousness must interact with the words of the participant recorded as fully and as accurately as possible.

Tape-recording offers other benefits as well. By preserving the words of the participants, researchers have their original data. If something is not clear in a transcript, the researchers can return to the source and check for accuracy. Later, if they are accused of mishandling their interview material, they can go back to their original sources to demonstrate their accountability to the data. In addition, interviewers can use tapes to study their interviewing techniques and improve upon them. Tape-recording also benefits the participants. The assurance that there is a record of what they have said to which they have access can give them more confidence that their words will be treated responsibly.

It may seem that the tape recorder could inhibit participants, but my experience is that they soon forget the device. Some interviewers, afraid that a tape recorder will affect the responses of their participants, use the smallest, least intrusive one they can find. Sometimes they sacrifice audio quality in doing so. I use a tape recorder with a separate microphone because I have found that some recorders with built-in microphones can muffle the sound and make transcribing an agony. I also do a test of how well the recorder is picking up the sound of the participant's and my voice before I start the actual interview. It is frustrating to interview someone for 4½ hours only to be unable to decipher the audiotape later. (See Yow, 1994, pp. 50–52, for an excellent presentation of many technical details interviewers must consider.)

TRANSCRIBING INTERVIEW TAPES

Transcribing interview tapes is time-consuming and potentially costly work. It can be facilitated by using a transcribing machine that has a foot pedal and earphones. Nonetheless it will normally take from 4 to 6 hours to transcribe a 90-minute tape. If possible, the initial transcriptions should be made using a computer-based word-processing program. Later, when researchers sort and refile material, having the interviews in computer files will prove highly efficient and labor saving. Interviewers who transcribe their own tapes come to know their interviews better, but the work is so demanding that they can easily tire and lose enthusiasm for interviewing as a research process.

Doctoral students ask me if there is a substitute for transcribing the entire interview tape. My response is yes, but not a good one. It is possible to listen to the tapes a number of times, pick out sections that seem important, and then transcribe just those. Although that approach is labor-saving, it is not desirable because it imposes the researcher's frame of reference on the interview data one step too early in the winnowing process. In working with the material, it is important that the researcher start with the whole (Briggs, 1986). Preselecting parts of the tapes to transcribe and omitting others tends to lead to premature judgments about what is important and what is not. Once the decision is made not to transcribe a portion of the tape, that portion of the interview is usually lost to the researcher. So although labor is saved in this alternative approach, the cost may be high.

The ideal solution is for the researcher to hire a transcriber. That, however, is expensive, and the job must be done well to be worth the effort. If interviewers can hire transcribers, or even if they do the transcriptions themselves, it is essential for them to develop explicit written instructions concerning the transcribing (Kvale, 1996). Writing out the instructions will improve the consistency of the process, encourage the researchers to think through all that is involved, and allow them to share their decision making with their readers at a later point. Although a transcript can be only a partial representation of the interview (Mishler, 1986), it can reflect the interview as fully as possible by being verbatim. In addition, the transcriber should make note of all the nonverbal signals, such as coughs, laughs, sighs, pauses, outside noises, telephone rings, and interruptions, that are recorded on the tape.

Both the interviewer and the transcriber must realize that decisions about where to punctuate the transcripts are significant. Participants do not speak in paragraphs or always clearly indicate the end of a sentence by voice inflection. Punctuating is one of the beginning points of the process of analyzing and interpreting the material (Kvale, 1996) and must be done thoughtfully. (For further discussion of transcription, see Alldred & Gillies, 2002, pp. 159–161; Mishler, 1991)

A detailed and careful transcript that re-creates the verbal and non-verbal material of the interview can be of great benefit to a researcher who may be studying the transcript months after the interview occurred. Note the care and precision with which the following section of an interview audiotape was transcribed. The interviewer is studying what it is like to be a communications major in a large university. Here she is asking the participant about financing her college education:

INTERVIEWER: Uhm, what does that experience mean to you?
PARTICIPANT: The fact that I spent so much money or that my parents like kind of rejected me?
INTERVIEWER: Both.
PARTICIPANT: Uhm, the fact that I spent so much money blows my mind because now I'm so poor and I'm. I can't believe I had so much, I mean I look back [slight pause] to the summer and the fall and [slight pause] I know where my money went. I mean, I was always down the Cape and I'd just spend at least $50 or $60 a night, you know, 3 or 4 nights a week. And then when I did an internship in town I was always driving in town, parking, saying "who cares" and I waitressed three shifts a week so I always had money in my pocket. So it was just, I always had money so, I never really cared and I never prepared for the future or never even considered that my parents wouldn't be there to foot the bill like they'd always been. And I wasn't really aware that they [pause] that they [slight pause and voice lowers] were becoming insulted. (Reproduced from Burke, 1990)

STUDYING, REDUCING, AND
ANALYZING THE TEXT

As one can see, in-depth interviewing generates an enormous amount of text. The vast array of words, sentences, paragraphs, and pages have to be reduced to what is of most significance and interest (McCracken, 1988; Miles & Huberman, 1984; Wolcott, 1990). Most important is that reducing the data be done inductively rather than deductively. That is, the researcher cannot address the material with a set of hypotheses to test or with a theory developed in another context to which he or she wishes to match the data (Glaser & Strauss, 1967). The researcher must come to the transcripts with an open attitude, seeking what emerges as important and of interest from the text.

At the same time, no interviewer can enter into the study of an interview as a clean slate (Rowan, 1981). All responses to a text are interactions between the reader and the text (Fish, 1980; Rosenblatt, 1982). That is why it is important that the researcher identify his or her interest in the subject and examine it to make sure that the interest is not infused with anger, bias, or prejudice. The interviewer must come to the transcript prepared to let the interview breathe and speak for itself.

Marking What Is of Interest in the Text

The first step in reducing the text is to read it and mark with brackets the passages that are interesting. The best description I have read of this aspect of the winnowing process is Judi Marshall's "Making Sense as a Personal Process" (1981). She acknowledges that what she can bring to the data is her sense of what is important as she reads the transcripts. She expresses confidence in being able to respond to meaningful "chunks" of transcript. She says that she recognizes them when she sees them and does not have to agonize over what level of semantic analysis she is doing. She affirms the role of her judgment in the process. In short, what is required in responding to interview text is no different from what is required in responding to other texts—a close reading plus judgment (Mostyn, 1985).

Marshall also talks about the dark side of this process: that time when, while working with interview data, you lose confidence in your ability to sort out what is important, you wonder if you are making it all up, and you feel considerable doubt about what you are doing. You become worried that you are falling into the trap of self-delusion, which Miles and

Huberman (1984) caution is the bane of those who analyze qualitative data. Marshall (1981) calls it an anxiety that you learn to live with.

It is important that researchers acknowledge that in this stage of the process they are exercising judgment about what is significant in the transcript. In reducing the material interviewers have begun to analyze, interpret, and make meaning of it. The interviewer-researchers can later check with the participants to see if what they have marked as being of interest and import seems that way to the participants. Although member-checking can inform a researcher's judgment, it cannot substitute for it (Lightfoot, 1983). That judgment depends on the researcher's experience, both in the past in general and in working with and internalizing the interviewing material; it may be the most important ingredient the researcher brings to the study (Marshall, 1981).

Although I can suggest some of the characteristics that make interviewing texts meaningful to me, there is no model matrix of interesting categories that one can impose on all texts. What is of essential interest is embedded in each research topic and will arise from each transcript. Interviewers must affirm their own ability to recognize it.

There are certain aspects of individual experience and social structure to which I respond when they appear. I am alert to conflict, both between people and within a person. I respond to hopes expressed and whether they are fulfilled or not. I am alert to language that indicates beginnings, middles, and ends of processes. I am sensitive to frustrations and resolutions, to indications of isolation and the more rare expressions of collegiality and community. Given the world in which we live, I am sensitive to the way issues of class, ethnicity, and gender play out in individual lives, and the way hierarchy and power affect people (Kanter, 1977). I do not, however, come to a transcript looking for these. When they are there, these and other passages of interest speak to me, and I bracket them.

Even when working with a research team, I give little instruction about marking what is of interest in a transcript other than to say, "Mark what is of interest to you as you read. Do not ponder about the passage. If it catches your attention, mark it. Trust yourself as a reader. If you are going to err, err on the side of inclusion." As you repeat the winnowing process, you can always exclude material; but materials once excluded from a text tend to become like unembodied thoughts that flee back to the stygian shadows of the computer file, and tend to remain there. (See Vygotsky, 1987, p. 210.) Despite my open instruction about marking transcripts, I have often found considerable overlap among my colleagues in what we have marked.

SHARING INTERVIEW DATA:
PROFILES AND THEMES

One goal of the researcher in marking what is of interest in the interview transcripts is to reduce and then shape the material into a form in which it can be shared or displayed (Miles & Huberman, 1984). Reducing the data is a first step in allowing the researchers to present their interview material and then to analyze and interpret it (Wolcott, 1994). It is one of the most difficult steps in the process because, inevitably, it means letting interview material go.

I have used two basic ways to share interview data. First, I have developed profiles of individual participants and grouped them in categories that made sense. Second, I have marked individual passages, grouped these in categories, and then studied the categories for thematic connections within and among them.

Rationale for Crafting Profiles

Although there is no right way to share interview data, and some researchers argue for less reliance on words and more on graphs, charts, and matrices (Miles & Huberman, 1984), I have found that crafting a profile or a vignette of a participant's experience is an effective way of sharing interview data and opening up one's interview material to analysis and interpretation. The idea comes from Studs Terkel's *Working* (1972).

Not all interviews will sustain display in the form of a profile. My experience is that only about one out of three interviews is complete and compelling enough to be shaped into a profile that has a beginning, a middle, and an end, as well as some sense of conflict and resolution. Other interviews may sustain what I call a vignette, which is a shorter narrative that usually covers a more limited aspect of a participant's experience.

A profile in the words of the participant is the research product that I think is most consistent with the process of interviewing. It allows us to present the participant in context, to clarify his or her intentions, and to convey a sense of process and time, all central components of qualitative analysis. (See Dey, 1993, pp. 30–39, for an excellent discussion of the question, "What is qualitative analysis?") We interview in order to come to know the experience of the participants through their stories. We learn from hearing and studying what the participants say. Although the interviewer can never be absent from the process, by crafting a profile in the participant's own words, the interviewer allows those words to reflect the person's consciousness.

Profiles are one way to solve the problem the interviewer has of how to share what he or she has learned from the interviews. The narrative form of a profile allows the interviewer to transform this learning into telling a story (Mishler, 1986). Telling stories, Mishler argues, is one major way that human beings have devised to make sense of themselves and their social world. I would add that telling stories is a compelling way to make sense of interview data. The story is both the participant's and the interviewer's. It is in the participant's words, but it is crafted by the interviewer from what the participant has said. Mishler provides an extended discussion of interviewing and its relationship to narratives as a way of knowing, and I strongly recommend it both for his own insights and the further reading that he suggests. (Also see Bruner, 1996, chaps. 6 & 7, for an important discussion of the role of narrative in constructing reality in the field of education.)

What others can learn from reading a profile of a participant is as diverse as the participants we interview, the profiles we craft and organize, and the readers who read them. I have found crafting profiles, however, to be a way to find and display coherence in the constitutive events of a participant's experience, to share the coherence the participant has expressed, and to link the individual's experience to the social and organizational context within which he or she operates.

If a researcher thinks that his or her interview material can sustain a profile that would bring a participant alive, offer insights into the complexities of what the researcher is studying, and is compelling and believable, taking the steps to craft a profile can be a rewarding way to share interview data. (See Locke, Silverman, & Spirduso, 2004, pp. 219–220.) Crafting a profile can bring an aesthetic component into reporting our research that makes both the researchers' and readers' work enriching, pleasurable, and at times touching to the spirit (Garman, 1994).

Steps in Crafting a Profile

Crafting profiles is a sequential process. Once you have read the transcript, marked passages of interest, and labeled those passages, make two copies of the marked and labeled transcript. (The labeling process is explained later in this chapter.) Using either the capabilities of a word-processing program, a dedicated qualitative analysis program, or even a pair of scissors, cut and file the marked passages on one copy of the transcripts into folders or computer files that correspond to the labels you devised for each passage. These excerpts will be used in the second, thematic way of sharing material. It is important never to cut up the original transcript because it serves throughout the study as a reference to which the researcher may turn for placing in context passages that have been excerpted.

From the other copy of the transcripts, select all the passages that you marked as important and put them together as a single transcript. Your resulting version may be one third to one half the length of the original three-interview transcript.

The next step is to read the new version, this time with a more demanding eye. It is very difficult to give up interview material. As you read, ask yourself which passages are the most compelling, those that you are just not willing to put aside. Underline them. Now you are ready to craft a narrative based on them.

One key to the power of the profile is that it is presented in the words of the participant. I cannot stress too much how important it is to use the first person, the voice of the participant, rather than a third-person transformation of that voice. To illustrate the point for yourself, take perhaps 30 seconds from one of your pilot interviews. First present the section verbatim. Then craft it into a mini-narrative using the first-person voice of the participant. Next try using your voice and describing the participant in the third person. It should become apparent that using the third-person voice distances the reader from the participant and allows the researcher to intrude more easily than when he or she is limited to selecting compelling material and weaving it together into a first-person narrative. Kvale (1996, p. 227) points out the temptation for researchers to expropriate and to use inappropriately their participants' experience for their own purposes. Using the first-person voice can help researchers guard against falling into this trap.

In creating profiles it is important to be faithful to the words of the participants and to identify in the narrative when the words are those of someone else. Sometimes, to make transitions between passages, you may wish to add your own words. Elsewhere you may want to clarify a passage. Each researcher can work out a system of notation to let the reader know when language not in the interview itself has been inserted. I place such language in brackets. I use ellipses when omitting material from a paragraph or when skipping paragraphs or even pages in the transcripts. In addition, I delete from the profile certain characteristics of oral speech that a participant would not use in writing–for example, repetitious "uhms," "ahs," "you knows," and other such idiosyncrasies that do not do the participant justice in a written version of what he or she has said.

Some might argue that researchers should make no changes in the oral speech of their participants when presenting it to an audience as a written document. I think, however, that unless the researcher is planning a semantic analysis or the subject of the interview itself is the language development of the participant, the claims for the realism of the oral speech are balanced by the researcher's obligation to maintain the dignity of the participant in presenting his or her oral speech in writing. (For further discussion of this issue see Blauner, 1987; Devault, 1990, pp. 106–107; Weiss, 1994, pp. 192–197.)

Normally, I try to present material in a profile in the order in which it came in the interviews. Material that means something in one context should not be transposed to another context that changes its meaning. However, if material in interview three, for example, fits with a part of the narrative based on interview two, I may decide to transpose that material, if doing so does not wrench it out of context and distort its meaning. In making all these decisions, I ask myself whether each is fair to the larger interview.

An important consideration in crafting a profile is to protect the identity of the participant if the written consent form calls for doing so. Even when transcribing the interview, use initials for all names that might identify the participant in case a casual reader comes across the transcript. In creating the profile itself, select a pseudonym that does justice to the participant. This is not an easy or a mechanical process. When choosing a pseudonym, take into consideration issues of ethnicity, age, and the context of the participant's life. Err on the side of understatement rather than overstatement. If a participant would be made vulnerable were his or her identity widely known, take additional steps to conceal it. For example, change the participant's geographical location, the details of his or her work—a physics teacher can become a science teacher—and other identifying facets of the person's experience. The extent to which an interviewer needs to resort to disguise is in direct relation to how vulnerable the person might be if identified. But the disguise must not distort what the participant has said in the interview. (See Lee, 1993, pp. 185–187, for further discussion of the issue of disguising participants' identity.)

The researcher must also be alert to whether he or she has made the participant vulnerable by the narrative itself. For example, Woods (1990) had to exercise extreme caution because, if her participants were identified, they might be fired from their teaching positions. Finally, the participant's dignity must always be a consideration. Participants volunteer to be interviewed but not to be maligned or incriminated by their own words. A function of the interviewing process and its products should be to reveal the participant's sense of self and worth.

Profiles as a Way of Knowing

I include in the Appendix two examples of profiles. The first is an edited version of a profile developed by Toon Fuderich (1995), who did her doctoral research on the child survivors of the Pol Pot era in Cambodia. She interviewed 17 refugees who had come to the United States to start a new life. The profile presented is of a participant called Nanda who was 28 at the time of her interview and worked part time in a human services agency. In a note to her paper, Fuderich indicated that in order to present the material clearly, she eliminated hesitations and repetitions in Nanda's speech. She also removed some of the idiosyncrasies of Nanda's speech and made grammatical corrections while at the same time remaining "respectful of the content and the intended meaning of the participant's words" (Fuderich, 1995).

I hesitated to include the profile of Nanda because I was afraid readers would think in-depth interviewing is only successful when it results in the kind of dramatic and heart-rending material Fuderich shared in Nanda's profile. I was concerned that potential researchers, especially doctoral candidates, would hesitate to try the process if their research areas seemed to them, in comparison, to be mundane.

As Nanda's profile reveals, in-depth interviewing is capable of capturing momentous, historical experiences. I wanted to both reveal that capability and share Fuderich's work, which seemed to me so compelling. However, in-depth interviewing research is perhaps even more capable of reconstructing and finding the compelling in the experiences of everyday life.

As a second example, therefore, I include in the Appendix an edited version of a profile developed by Marguerite Sheehan (1989). (For other examples of such profiles, see Seidman, 1985.) This profile resulted from a pilot study Sheehan conducted of the experience of day-care providers who have stayed in the field for a long time. (See Chapter 3 for a description of her interview structure.)

The profile presented is of a participant, Betty, who is a family day-care provider. She takes care of six children in her home every day. Most of the children are in "protective slots," that is, their day care is paid for by the state. Their parents are often required to leave them in care because the children either have been or are at risk of being abused or neglected.

Sheehan presented a version of this profile to our seminar on In-Depth Interviewing and Issues in Qualitative Research. In her final comments, she wrote:

> Betty had many other things to say that I was not able to fit into this report. She talked quite a bit about how her daughter and husband were involved in the Family Day Care whether through their physical presence or their interest in the children. She told me more stories about individual children and families that she worked with. I was impressed with how she identified at different times with both the children and the parents and how she had to let go while still remaining involved with them. Betty was often nervous and worried that she was not saying the "right thing." She told me that this was the first time that anyone had asked her about the meaning in her work. (Sheehan, 1989)

Betty's profile tells an important story in her own words. It may not have the life-and-death drama of Nanda's profile, but it captures compellingly, I think, the struggle of a day-care provider from which anyone interested in day care can learn.

As both Fuderich and Sheehan pursued their research, they interviewed additional participants. If they had chosen to do so, they could have presented a series of profiles grouped together around organizing topics. In addition to the profiles' speaking powerfully for themselves, the researchers would have been able to explore and comment on the salient issues within individual profiles and point out connections among profiles. For example, in the profile of Betty, the issues of how people come to the work of day care, the preparation they have, the support they are given, the effect of the low status and genderized nature of the work, the relatively unexplored subject of working with the parents, and the issue of child abuse, to name several, are raised. In Nanda's profile, issues inherent in the traumas of history, being a refugee, learning English as a second language, and the tensions and complexities of acculturation are raised, among others.

Each researcher would be able to make explicit what she has learned about those subjects through the presentation of the profiles and also through connecting those profiles to the experience of others in her sample. By telling Betty's story of her everyday work in her own words,

Sheehan is setting the stage for her readers to learn about the issues involved in providing day care through the experiences of a person deeply involved in that work. By telling Nanda's story, Fuderich is inviting readers to both bear witness and begin to understand the factors influencing resilience among those who, as children, survived the Cambodian genocide, which is the subject of her dissertation study.

MAKING AND ANALYZING THEMATIC CONNECTIONS

A more conventional way of presenting and analyzing interview data than crafting profiles is to organize excerpts from the transcripts into categories. The researcher then searches for connecting threads and patterns among the excerpts within those categories and for connections between the various categories that might be called themes. In addition to presenting profiles of individuals, the researcher, as part of his or her analysis of the material, can then present and comment upon excerpts from the interviews thematically organized.

During the process of reading and marking the transcripts, the researcher can begin to label the passages that he or she has marked as interesting. After having read and indicated interesting passages in two or three participants' interviews, the researcher can pause to consider whether they can be labeled. What is the subject of the marked passages? Are there words or a phrase that seems to describe them, at least tentatively? Is there a word within the passage itself that suggests a category into which the passage might fit? In Sheehan's transcript, some of the labels for the passages included in the Appendix might be "background of provider," "support groups," "impact on family," "abuse," and "parents."

The process of noting what is interesting, labeling it, and putting it into appropriate files is called "classifying" or, in some sources, "coding" data. (See Dey, 1993, p. 58, for a critique of the term *coding* as applied to qualitative research.) Computer programs are available that will help classify, sort, file, and reconnect interview data. By telling the computer what to look for, the program can scan large amounts of data quickly and sort material into categories according to the directions.

For those who choose to work with either a dedicated analytical program or even a word-processing program, I suggest caution in doing significant coding or editing on screen. I recommend working first on a paper copy and then transferring the work to the computer. My experience is that there is a significant difference between what one sees in a text presented on paper and the same text shown on screen, and that one's response is different, too. I have learned, for example, that it is foolish of me to edit on screen, because I invariably miss issues that are easily evident to me when I work with a paper copy. I would not recommend relying on reading an interview text on screen for the process of categorizing material. Something in the mediums of screen and paper affects the message the viewer retrieves (see McLuhan, 1965, for an early and influential commentary on this process).

At this point in the reading, marking, and labeling process it is important to keep labels tentative. Locking in categories too early can lead to dead ends. Some of the categories will work out. That is, as the researcher continues to read and mark interview transcripts, other passages will come up that seem connected to the same category. On the other hand, some categories that seemed promising early in the process will die out. New ones may appear. Categories that seemed separate and distinct will fold into each other. Others may remain in flux almost until the end of the study.[1] (See Charmaz, 1983, for an excellent description of the process of coding; also Davis, 1984.)

In addition to labeling each marked passage with a term that places it in a category, researchers should also label each passage with a notation system that will designate its original place in the transcript. (Dey, 1993, points out that many dedicated analytical computer programs will do this automatically.) I use, for example, the initials of the participant, a Roman numeral for the number of the interview in the three-interview sequence, and Arabic numbers for the page number of the transcript on which the passage occurs. Later, when working with the material and considering an excerpt taken from its original context, the researcher may want to check the accuracy of the text and replace it in its full context, even going back to the audiotape itself. The labeling of each excerpt allows such retracing.

The next step is to file those excerpts either in computer files under the name of the assigned category or in folders. Some excerpts might fit reasonably into more than one file. Make copies of those and file in the multiple files that seem appropriate.

After filing all the marked excerpts, reread all of them file by file. Start sifting out the ones that now seem very compelling, setting aside the ones that seem at this stage to be of less interest. At this point, the researcher is in what Rowan (1981) calls a "dialectical" process with the material (p. 134). The participants have spoken, and now the interviewer is responding to their words, concentrating his or her intuition and intellect on the process. What emerges is a synthesis of what the participant has said and how the researcher has responded.

Some commentators regard this sorting and culling as an entirely intuitive process (Tagg, 1985). It is important, however, that researchers also try to form and articulate their criteria for the winnowing and sorting process. By doing so, they give their readers a basis for understanding the process the researchers used in reducing the mass of words to more manageable proportions.

I do not begin to read the transcripts with a set of categories for which I want to find excerpts. The categories arise out of the passages that I have marked as interesting. On the other hand, when I reflect on the types of material that arouse my interest, it is clear that some patterns are present, that I have certain predispositions I bring to my reading of the transcripts.

When working with excerpts from interview material, I find myself selecting passages that connect to other passages in the file. In a way, quantity starts to interact with quality. The repetition of an aspect of experience that was already mentioned in other passages takes on weight and calls attention to itself.

I notice excerpts from a participant's experience that connect to each other as well as to passages from other participants. Sometimes excerpts connect to the literature on the subject. They stand out because I have read about the issue from a perspective independent of my interviewing.

Some passages are told in a striking manner or highlight a dramatic incident. Those are perhaps the most troublesome for me. They are attractive because of their style or the sheer drama of the incident, but I know that I have to be careful about such passages. The dramatic can be confused with the pervasive. The researcher has to judge whether the particular dramatic incident is idiosyncratic or characteristic (Mostyn, 1985).

Some passages stand out because they are contradictory and seem decisively inconsistent with others. It is tempting to put those aside. These in particular, however, have to be kept in the foreground, lest researchers exercise their own biased subjectivity, noticing and using only materials that support their own opinions (Kvale, 1996, p. 212; Locke, Silverman, & Spirduso, 2004, pp. 222–223). The researcher has to try to understand their importance in the face of the other data he or she has gathered (Miles & Huberman, 1984).

The process of working with excerpts from participants' interviews, seeking connections among them, explaining those connections, and building interpretative categories is demanding and involves risks. The danger is that the researcher will try to force the excerpts into categories, and the categories into themes that he or she already has in mind, rather than let them develop from the experience of the participants as represented in the interviews. The reason an interviewer spends so much time talking to participants is to find out what *their* experience is and the meaning *they* make of it, and then to make connections among the experiences of people who share the same structure. Rowan (1981) stresses the inappropriateness of force-fitting the words of participants into theories derived from other sources.

There is no substitute for total immersion in the data. It is important to try to articulate criteria for marking certain passages as notable and selecting some over others in order for the process to have public credibility. It is also important to affirm your judgment as a researcher. You have done the interviewing, studied the transcripts, and read the related literature; you have mentally lived with and wrestled with the data, and now you need to analyze them. As Judi Marshall (1981) says, your feeling of rightness and coherence about the process of working with the data is important. It is your contribution as the researcher.

INTERPRETING THE MATERIAL

Interpreting is not a process researchers do only near the end of the project. Even as interviewers question their participants, tentative interpretations may begin to influence the path of their questioning. Marking passages that are of interest, labeling them, and grouping them is analytic work that has within it the seeds of interpretation. Crafting a profile is an act of analysis, as is presenting and commenting upon excerpts arranged in categories. Both processes lay the ground for interpretation. (I am using Wolcott's [1994] distinction between the words *analysis* and *interpretation.* I think Wolcott offers a solid approach to working with interview data in his thoughtful explication of the terms *description, analysis,* and *interpretation.* In this book, I have used the phrase *sharing the data* instead of Wolcott's *description.*)

In some ways, it is tempting to let the profiles and the categorized, thematic excerpts speak for themselves. But another step is appropriate. Researchers must ask themselves what they have learned from doing the interviews, studying the transcripts, marking and labeling them, crafting profiles, and organizing categories of excerpts. What connective threads are there among the experiences of the participants they interviewed? How do they understand and explain these connections? What do they understand now that they did not understand before they began the interviews? What surprises have there been? What confirmations of previous instincts? How have their interviews been consistent with the literature? How inconsistent? How have they gone beyond?

Charmaz (1983), Glaser and Strauss (1967), and Maxwell (1996) address these questions with a practical suggestion: When you have identified passages that are important but the category in which they fall seems undefined or its significance is unclear, write a memorandum about those passages. Through your writing about them, about how they were picked, about what they mean to you, the properties and import of the category may become clear. If you write such memoranda about each of the categories you have developed and about the profiles you have crafted, the process of writing about them will lead you to discover what it is you find important in them both individually and relative to others that you have developed.

Much of what you learn may be tentative, suggesting further research. In the early stages of our study of student teachers and mentors (Fischetti, Santilli, & Seidman, 1988; O'Donnell et al., 1989), we began to see evidence in the language of the student teachers we interviewed that tracking in schools was affecting how they were learning to become teachers. That led O'Donnell (1990) to conceptualize a dissertation study on the impact of tracking on learning to become a teacher.

The last stage of interpretation, then, consistent with the interview process itself, asks researchers what meaning they have made of their work. In the course of interviewing, researchers asked the participants what their experience meant to them. Now they have the opportunity to respond to the same question. In doing so they might review how they came to their research, what their research experience was like, and, finally, what it means to them. How do they understand it, make sense of it, and see connections in it?

Some of what researchers learn may lead them to propose connections among events, structures, roles, and social forces operating in people's lives. Some researchers would call such proposals *theories* and urge theory building as the purpose of research (Fay, 1987). My own feeling is that although the notion of grounded theory generated by Glaser and Strauss (1967) offered qualitative researchers a welcome rationale for their inductive approach to research, it also served to inflate the term *theory* to the point that it has lost some of its usefulness. (See Dey, 1993, pp. 51–52, for a useful critique of the casual use of the word *theory*.)

The narratives we shape of the participants we have interviewed are necessarily limited. Their lives go on; our presentations of them are framed and reified. Betty, whose profile is in the Appendix, may be still working out her relationship to child care. Nanda is still living out her life in the United States. Moreover, the narratives that we present are a function of our interaction with the participants and their words. Although my experience suggests that a number of people reading Betty's or Nanda's transcripts separately would nevertheless develop similar narratives, we still have to leave open the possibility that other interviewers and crafters of profiles would have told a different story. (See Fay, 1987, pp. 166–174.) So, as illuminating as in-depth interviews can be, as compelling as the stories are that they can tell and the themes they can highlight, we still have to bear in mind that Heisenberg's principle of indeterminacy pervades our work, as it does the work of physicists (Polanyi, 1958). We have to allow considerable tolerance for uncertainty (Bronowski, 1973) in the way we report what we have learned from our research.

Every research method has its limits and its strengths. In-depth interviewing's strength is that through it we can come to understand the details of people's experience from their point of view. We can see how their individual experience interacts with powerful social and organizational forces that pervade the context in which they live and work, and we can discover the interconnections among people who live and work in a shared context.

In-depth interviewing has not led me to an easy confidence in the possibilities of progressive reform through research (Bury, 1932; Fay, 1987). It has led me to a deeper understanding and appreciation of the amazing intricacies and, yet, coherence of people's experiences. It has also led me to a more conscious awareness of the power of the social and organizational context of people's experience. Interviewing has provided me with a deeper understanding of the issues, structures, processes, and policies that imbue participants' stories. It has also given me a fuller appreciation of the complexities and difficulties of change. Most important and almost always, interviewing continues to lead me to respect the participants, to relish the understanding that I gain from them, and to take pleasure in sharing their stories.

NOTE

1. The number of themes that emerge into prominence in an interview study has implications for the organization of a dissertation. While the format of a dissertation is in the purview of dissertation committees, I think it reasonable

to suggest that interviewing studies, so rich in words, may not lend themselves to the conventional five-chapter dissertation. That format was developed with quantitative research in mind. In the five-chapter format, the first chapter introduces the problem or issue and its significance. The second chapter reviews the related research. The third outlines the research method used in the study. The fourth chapter reports on the results or findings, which in a quantitatively-based study are often numeric in form. The fifth chapter offers a discussion of the results.

In an interview study, researchers may want to present themes that have evolved from their study of the transcript as the focus of their findings or results. Instead of one chapter of findings, researchers may decide to present each major theme, illustrated by the words of their participants, in its own chapter. (See Cook, 2004, for an example.) Alternatively, it might be possible to connect two or three lesser but related themes in a chapter and perhaps illuminate them with supporting profiles or vignettes. So, an interviewing study might have two or three chapters that replace the conventional fourth chapter of results and findings. In a concluding chapter, researchers interpret and discuss their findings, and may reflect upon what they have learned and what the interviews mean to them.

Two Profiles

NANDA—A CAMBODIAN SURVIVOR
OF THE POL POT ERA
(Toon Fuderich)

Before the war, . . . we had a very large extended family . . . a lot of aunts, uncles, cousins, and grandparents. I am one of four children. I have an older brother and a younger brother and sister. My family was quite well-off. My father had his own business; my mother owned a grocery store; my paternal grandparents owned a flour mill. My father was well respected in our village. He was a handsome and intelligent man who valued education highly. He always told us about the importance of getting an education.

I was 8 years old when Pol Pot took over Cambodia . . . forced labor camps were established throughout the country. People were forced to leave their home to work in these camps. When the war broke out, Khmer Rouge soldiers came to our village. They told us that they came to free us from the oppressive government. They told us not to worry about anything and that everything will be fine. But nothing was fine. It was all a lie. They killed innocent people. The educated professionals like doctors, businessmen, teachers were the first to be killed. It was just horrible.

Every day the soldiers organized a meeting to re-educate the villagers. The meeting usually runs from 6 A.M. to 6 P.M. Everyone had to attend except for those who were gravely ill. . . . One day just before my father left for the meeting, a group of soldiers came for my father. My mother was already at the meeting. I was the only one left at home at the time. They entered our house. Ransacked the whole place (long pause) took everything . . . Then my father was led outside, his hands were tied behind his back. I was so frightened, but decided to follow them.

I hid behind a cupboard and tried to peer through a small crack to see my father. The soldiers accused my father of betraying his country. My father kept saying to them "I love my country. I have children. I love my country" and the soldiers kept berating him, yelling at him, accusing him of working for the government and hiding guns in his house. A young soldier no more than 10 years old put a gun on my father's forehead. I was terrified. Then I saw an older soldier winking at the young soldier, signaling him to pull a trigger. And that was it. They killed my father. They shot him. I saw it with my own eyes. I couldn't move. I was too scared to cry. I sat froze behind my hiding place. I was alone. I was the only who saw this happen. I was numb. I couldn't feel anything. . . . I tell you I was so numb. After they shot him they took out a big machine gun and started to shoot at his already dead body, his chest, head, legs. They took his wallet and other valuables. I saw everything, but I felt nothing. It was awful.

When I got over the shock, I ran to my mother and told her about what happened to my father. My mother was 9 months pregnant at the time. She was crying and sobbing. She kept asking the soldiers why they killed my father. One soldier looked at her and pointed a gun at her stomach. He said, "Don't cry, my friend. Your husband is a bad man. He betrayed his country. Tomorrow I will find a nice man to marry you." My mother kept on crying, crouching down to the ground. I couldn't cry. I could not feel anything. I asked my older brother to take me to grandmother's house. It was not until I reached her house that I began to cry. I couldn't stop crying. My grandmother was annoyed, so she said to me, "Why are you crying so much? Did someone kill your father?" I looked at her and said, "Yes." And I told her what happened. My grandmother, when she realized, she just fainted.

My brother and I then went back to our house. My mother was still crying. Neighbors and friends came to see us. They were sad and shocked but couldn't do anything to help. They were scared [of the soldiers]. They felt bad but there was nothing they could do to help. My mother asked the soldiers if she could properly bury my father but they refused. They told us that my father's body should be left for the dogs to eat or we can throw him into the stream to feed the fish. My mom cried so much. We all cried. I will never forget this. Eventually, the soldiers allowed us to bury my father. We used a straw mat to wrap his body before burying him.

A few days after my father died, the soldiers ordered all of the villagers to leave the village. They told us that we were only going to be gone for a few days but . . . we . . . never got to return to our home. We took nothing with us. They led us to a work camp at the edge of the forest. My mom was very pregnant. It was hard for her. There were no shelters, no nothing. Our family and extended families were together at this point.

We gathered some wood to make temporary shelters for us. Shortly after we arrived at this work camp my mother went into labor. There was no midwife. My grandmother asked around but found no one. Somehow she managed to deliver the baby. After the delivery, my mother was so exhausted that she became unconscious for 2 hours. The baby survived. My mother survived. It was a good thing that she managed to live.

After giving birth, my mother had to go directly to work in the rice field. My grandparents looked after the baby. Older people were assigned to take care of younger children during this time. Children from 5 years old up had to work. The children and parents worked separately. Husbands and wives had to be separated. There was a lot of killing and shooting. I saw a man killed because he refused to be separated from his wife and children. Yeah, they shot him. So many people died of sickness and starvation too.

After a year, they moved us to another work camp. At this camp I was separated from my mother. I had to go live in the children's camp. Here, they tried to brainwash us, turning us against our parents, telling us to spy on them. They told us that we don't have to respect our parents anymore and that giving birth to a child is a natural life process. We don't have to be faithful to our parents. They said that children are precious and special and our lives worth more than adults'. But it wasn't true. They killed children too.

While separated from my mother I was miserable. I missed her so much. More than once I tried to run away to join her at her campsite but they found me. They tied me up and punished me, told me not to do it again. They told me that my life belongs to the public now and I have to contribute.

I cried all the time. I missed my father so much. I was hoping that he will reincarnate. I waited for him but he never came back. I asked my mother about the reincarnation but she said my father is not coming back. I was upset with her. I cried and she cried. I suffered so much. I had very little food to eat. Sometimes I was so hungry that I would eat anything, leaves, raw snails, crabs or anything I caught while working in the field. I got sick all the time. The children fought with each other a lot. One day I had a very high fever and couldn't get up to work. One kid came to me, pulled my hair and dragged me to work. . . . Yeah, kids ruled one another. The stronger ones were the ones who had power.

I was so thin. My belly always swollen. We didn't eat well. Once a year maybe the soldiers would cook us rice and soup. I remembered one time during this so-called feast I ate too much that I nearly died. I could not move. You know, my stomach was full but my mouth was hungry. Two kids died from overeating. . . .

Since we had no food to eat, we had to move on. We gathered what was left and headed towards the Thai border. We walked for days without food. I had to carry my 3-year-old brother on my back. He was so heavy that I wanted to kill him (small laugh). . . . By the time we arrived at the border everyone was so tired we just flopped on the ground. There was an intense fighting between the Vietnamese troops and Khmer Rouge soldiers. We slept amid bombing and gun firing. Bullets were flying over our heads. There was nothing we could do. The next day we moved to another camp. At this camp, refugee relief organizations gave us some food and sheets of plastic to make shelter for ourselves. We searched for my older brother but couldn't find him. Someone told us that he joined Khmer Srai [Free Khmer].

Life in this camp was not easy. We slept on the ground. It was during the rainy season so it rained all the time. Sometimes I slept with half of my body lying in the water. But nothing really mattered anymore . . . live or die. We just let it go. My mom usually stayed up to guard us while we slept. I worked all the time, fetching water for people. They paid me a little bit of money. I earned 30 bahts a day [$1]. I saved money to buy things for my family.

After a few months my older brother reunited with us. We were relieved but we had to move again because the fighting at the border intensified. It was getting too dangerous to live here.

We had to make it to the holding center for refugees in Thailand in order to be safe. We walked, ran, and dodged. We had to be careful not to step on mine fields. Luckily, the United Nations truck picked us up on the way. Everything was in such a rush. My older brother couldn't make it on the bus so we lost him again. Everyone on the truck was crying asking for their family members. It was very sad and confusing.

We made it to Thailand finally. The UN put us into a refugee holding center. I was happy that we managed to stay alive. The UN gave us some materials to make our own shelter . . . you know . . . poles and plastic sheets. It was a break but I was still in shock. The UN gave us canned sardines, rice, and cooking oil. It was good (laugh). Life at the holding center was not bad. Sometimes I sneaked outside the camp with some adults to buy food from the Thai market. We are not supposed to do that but I did it anyway, out of curiosity. I got caught once and was put in jail for 3 days. They cut my hair off. My mother spent 3 days crying, looking for me everywhere. She thought I was killed.

I attended an elementary school in the camp and learned Khmer . . . I enjoyed living there. People, Thai people are helpful and nice. I made some Thai friends there. But only for 6 months because we had to move to another camp . . . just as we began to feel comfortable, the UN decided to close the camp down so we had to move back to the first refugee camp again. It was not easy you know moving back and forth. Sometimes it was unbearable.

When we came back, I attended a class in public health that was offered by a relief organization. I studied and passed the test. Afterward, I went to work in a camp day-care center. I met my future husband there. We worked together. During this time I worked and studied all the time . . . later on I took another job as a translator at the camp hospital. It was very hard work, but important work. I helped the foreign doctors and nurses tend the wounded Khmer soldiers. There were truckloads of them coming to the hospital each day. It was very painful for me to see so much suffering.

One good thing that happened while we were in the first camp was that we reunited with my brother. He was working for the American embassy as a translator. We submitted the application applying for a resettlement in the United States and were accepted. Shortly after we were sent to a transit camp to learn some English. We spent 1 month before leaving for another transit camp in the Philippines. The camp in the Philippines was beautiful. It was right on the ocean. Plenty of food and fruits. People were nice and friendly. I relaxed and learned English. While waiting in the Philippines, I married my colleague with whom I worked at the camp day-care center.

Shortly after I got married, my mother and siblings left for Florida. I stayed behind with my husband. We left the Philippines for the USA in 1984. Coming from the war zone where I saw nothing but cruelty and destruction I was overwhelmed by everything I saw in the U.S. Everything is different. I couldn't understand the language.

People speak too fast for me to understand them and my accent is too difficult for them to understand me. So what are you going to do? It was extremely frustrating. I remembered feeling depressed, lonely and confused all the time. I didn't want to be here. I didn't know why I had to be here. I couldn't stop thinking about my past, about Cambodia.

Learning English was a real struggle for me. My accent is so bad that people always have a hard time understanding my English. I tried so hard to learn English because I know that I have to live here for the rest of my life. I had to do something. I attended an ESL class. I can speak better English but still have problems with my accent and pronunciation.

Living with my husband's adopted family was hard. They don't know me so they don't understand me. I don't have anyone but my husband to turn to . . . I cried all the time because I felt sad, lost, and unloved. I lost hope in my life. Then I found out that I was pregnant. My pregnancy changed everything . . . for the better. I think because it gave me strength and some hope. I knew that I had to do something. I had to change a course in my life. I have come this far I must continue. I thought about my time in Cambodia during the war when I had nothing to eat. I could not do much there but at least here I have food to eat and roof over my head. I can make it here and I have to take advantage of it. I knew that I had to get some education before I can move on to do something. I had to pick myself up.

I enrolled in the GED class. My first day in class was not a pleasant one. Most of my classmates are teen mothers like myself. I did not feel welcome. They laughed at my accent. One time the teacher asked me to read a paragraph in the book. I must have sounded very funny that a classmate laughed so hard that she fell off her chair. I was so humiliated . . . so angry. My teacher reprimanded her for doing that. It hurt so much. The girl just couldn't understand where I come from. It became obvious to me that I was an outsider. I was not a part of their circle of friends. I didn't know who Michael Jackson is. I didn't know any of the talk-show hosts on television so I couldn't participate in their conversation. I was always on the outside.

After the birth of my daughter I studied at home. A tutor came to my home to help me with my homework. My husband and I moved out of my in-laws' house . . . it took me 3 years to finally pass the GED test. It was quite an accomplishment. The local paper wrote an article about me. At the graduation ceremony I was walking on air. I was happy and proud of myself, but at the same time felt very sad because my father and mother were not with me on this very important day of my life.

After I got my GED I applied for a job. I was hired as a translator. I worked as a translator for a while. After a year or so I asked my supervisor if I can do some counseling. She let me. I was very nervous the first time I did it. I told my client to take it easy if I made a mistake. My boss sent me to Boston for additional training in nutrition and counseling. I also took two courses in nutrition and counseling at the community college. I worked very hard all the time. Homework was always difficult. It always took me a long time to complete my homework assignments. It was not easy but I enjoyed learning. I am certified to do nutritional counseling and have been working for 8 years now.

In 1989 I was diagnosed of having a molar pregnancy. My placenta kept growing but there was no baby inside. The doctor performed surgery and tried to clean it up but it didn't work. It got so serious that the doctor told me I may die. Can you imagine someone told you that you only have a few more months to live. It was very scary. My daughter was only 3 years old. I went to a hospital in Boston for chemotherapy treatment. Chemotherapy made me feel really sick. After each dosage I felt sick for 2 weeks. I couldn't walk, eat or help myself. You could not breathe well after chemotherapy treatment. I was so miserable that several times I wanted to kill myself. I was totally crazy. Every time I heard the word *chemotherapy* I cried. I took 6 months of chemotherapy to get rid of the irregular hormone. I am fine now but after the chemotherapy I am not the same person anymore. I am moody, impatient, and get tired easily. I have to take it very easy.

Now I only work part-time. I try to spend a lot of time with my child. I try to enjoy my life. In the past I didn't have time to think about having a good time because I always had to struggle to survive. Being close to death twice I knew that anything can happen. I lost my childhood to war. I nearly died of sickness. Now I have a chance to live; I have to enjoy it.

Life is too short you know. Here today gone tomorrow. First I thought I wanted to continue with school but I realized that I could not possibly put up with the pressure. It's OK. I like where I am now. I have my family.

I keep minimum contact with the Cambodian community here because the more I get involved the more headache I get. Cambodians used to love each other but here [it is different]. I think a lot of people here still have not yet come to terms with their past. They are disturbed and have a hard time coping. I had to work very hard to overcome my painful past, but some people just don't know how to do that. . . . They accuse me of being too American. I don't know what that means. I am not American. I don't know, really, who I am, but I like where I am. It is confusing sometimes you know, not really fit in anywhere. I don't know much about Cambodian culture because I spent most of my childhood dodging bullets. I try to learn about my culture now so I can teach my kids. Yes, it is funny, not knowing much about your own roots.

In general, I think I am pretty lucky. I have a job that I like, a supportive husband, and two lovely kids. My colleagues are great. . . . I try not to think too much about my past. But how can one forget the unforgettable? I remember it. In fact I am trying to write a book about it. I write in English, though it may not make sense at all because my English is poor. I do it anyway because writing helps relieve my pain. Maybe someone out there can learn from my story. I remember everything that happened to me during the war but it doesn't bother me anymore because I am looking forward . . . want a future. My past is very dark and there is nothing I can do to change it. I can not undo it . . . no. I can only go forward. I have to be strong for my children. Life is full of surprises. Today we are laughing and feel good but tomorrow who knows. Nothing is permanent I learn. I learn also that I can depend on no one but myself. When I am strong people recognize me. When I am weak people step on me. I think I am strong and prepared. If something very bad happens to me tomorrow I will not fall apart. The worst things already happened to me, you know, sickness, war. I think I can handle it. (Fuderich, 1995)

BETTY—A LONG-TIME DAY CARE PROVIDER
(Marguerite Sheehan)

It's my 9th year [of day care]. It's a long time. I only wanted to do it for a year, see how my daughter would feel about it. . . . I had a different idea of day care. It was more or less like one or two kids come and play. I didn't realize how much work was really involved. But then it became a routine. We eat, we go to the park. There were two ladies in the area who also did child care, that I found out went every morning to the playground. That's how I met a lot of other people. I found out things I never knew before about child care and certain things to do with a certain age. It helped me a great deal with my own daughter. It was good for her. Even then I was taking protective children, so it taught her that not everyone lived the way we did. It helped my husband too. It helped the whole family.

I grew up as an only child [adopted at infancy] but we lived in an apartment house and there were always kids around me. I always took care of kids. . . . My mother never worked. There was that thing with my father: A woman stayed home, takes care of the children and the house. Nothing else, though we could have used the money. I'm sure I bothered my mother a lot of times. She wished she could have gone out and gotten a job instead of staying home with me. But after a while I guess she didn't mind anymore.

[Now] it's funny when kids turn around to me and say, "How come you aren't working? How come you don't have a job?" I try to explain to them, I am working. I'm doing day care. [They say] "No, you don't. How come they are giving you money? You don't even work."

A lot of people [in the neighborhood] know you after a while. "Here comes that lady with all the kids." They know you and help you cross the street. I think they appreciate me but I hear all the time people telling me, "Oh my God, how can you do that? I couldn't do it. Six little kids. God, I'd rather work in a factory!" I do get looks sometimes when I go to the store. I don't care. I couldn't care less. It doesn't bother me. . . .

There are times when I say, "I can't do this anymore. I've got to quit. I'm going crazy." And then you get a child that didn't talk at all when he came, or was really shy and then all of a sudden you get a big hug. That makes me feel good because I know I accomplished something too. Maybe it took a long time but he finally came out of his shell. It makes me feel real good. . . .

Somebody asked me a while back, "Wouldn't you like to do something else? What do you see? What is in the future? You know, no promotions." For me there is a promotion. When a kid comes and finally talks or gives you that big hug or cries by the time they have to leave, it really makes me feel good. That's my promotion. It sounds corny but it's true.

[The children] are not going to be the way you want them to be like, talking or laughing all the time. . . . I had one particular case where the child told me he was going to kick my butt, and he told me how, with a knife! [He said] "That's how you cut up people." He did come back the next day; in his sneakers was a little can opener that you hang on a key chain. He showed it to me. [He said again], "That's how you cut up people." It really scared me. [I thought] this kid has got to go, he's dangerous. But he really isn't. A lot of the time it isn't the kids at all. It's the parents. They [the kids] have to act it out somehow.

I think [day care] a lot of the times really helps the parents. If the child's away for certain hours of the day it gives them a break and hopefully things will go better for them when they realize there is a break. When you get to know the [parent] after a while, sit down and have a cup of coffee, lots of parents sat and cried and told me what happened. Starting from when they were children, or what happened the night before. Sometimes you could really feel for them. . . .

Some protective parents don't really want to deal with me. You can tell. They either don't let me know when the kid is missing; [they say] "So what's the big deal, you don't really need to know." Probably they feel threatened by me. What if the kid does tell me something in the morning that I have to report . . . the parents have needs too. Some of them are really alone. And then I have parents who have kids who weren't abused or neglected. . . . I could say the wrong thing and set them off. I'm not a professional . . .

We have a support group where we meet once a month. The support group consists of four providers and a social worker. We can sit and discuss problems we have with the kids [and ask] what somebody else would do about it. I think that is why a lot of providers quit. Especially the ones who are isolated. There is nobody you can talk to. You talk to little kids all day. It happens to me too. I'll go to a birthday party and I see myself going to the little kids instead of the adults. I feel comfortable there. Sometimes you don't know what to say to adults because you are so alone sometimes. That's why the support group is good . . . . It's only 1½ or 2 hours long, but you hear someone else. Just to sit and talk to another adult makes you feel really good.

I have to keep a log on each of the children. You hear all those things now lately about providers being accused of abusing one of the kids. It really helps to [be able] to go back a couple of months. [To be able to] say, "Wait a minute, this child wasn't even in" [that day] or whatever. That's what I like about a [day-care] system too. You can go back and I know they will support you. I mean [if] somebody doesn't know you [after] 9 years, they never know you. . . .

When it happened to me, when the parent called me up I felt angry. I think I would have done something very stupid if the person [had been] in the house. It had started off with, "The child is coming home with bruises every day and I want to know" [what's happening]. She was cursing on the phone. And then it got worse. [She said] "My lawyer wants to meet you."

Finally I said, "Look, I've been doing this for such a long time. I've never abused anybody." I was really angry. And I said to myself, "I'm crazy to do this kind of job." I still don't know what happened with the bruises. The bruise was made out to be as though the kid was black and blue from top to bottom. There were two, not even the size of a penny, around the knees. It's probably from crawling. I don't deny the bruises, but I do deny that I'm hurting someone. It did make me angry. I think that's why a lot of people quit. It's just the idea that what if they do believe the other party? What if they close you up? Will they do an investigation? What happens in the meantime?

Maybe I triggered it off because the baby was really sick. I kept telling her to take her to the doctor. I said to the social worker that I want that baby to be seen by a doctor or she doesn't return to day care. It happened on Friday, and Monday I was called. They were threatening me

I think, not knowing that I really meant well for the baby, plus for the protection of the other kids. . . .

A few years ago, my husband would have said, "That's it. You've got to quit!" Now he says, "Calm down. They're going to be calm by tomorrow." I can talk to my kids or talk to him. That helps, if you have someone to talk to. . . .

There was one case where I ended up taking the younger child into foster care. I think we would still have her but there were family problems. The father interfering, threatening me, and it became really too much to deal with. When I do see her, I feel awfully bad, like I should have kept her. But we had a choice to make then. [It was] even to the point where my daughter was frightened. She received a call and she got afraid and then we had to make a choice. We couldn't live in fear. I didn't want my daughter to live in fear. . . .

I guess I feel good that several kids really trust me. [They have with me] a place they can come to, a routine. Also they come and tell me certain stuff. [There were] two mothers who felt threatened. One mother stopped by. She told me she had a little bit of a problem with her husband. She sat there where she would never have come before. So it's both children and parents that begin to trust. . . .

My kids all come by bus. It's hard for a kid, being 3 years old. . . . All of a sudden that big bus comes which is already scary. Your mom puts you on and off you go. You don't know whether you'll ever go home. Some of my kids were in foster care before coming to day care. They don't know if they are going home or not.

It's really hard [when the kids leave family day care]. I try to tell parents to make sure the kid comes on the last day. Plus for a few days I tell the kids that one is going to leave for whatever reason. And then the kid doesn't come back, I don't feel it's right for that child or for the others because nobody knows what's really going on. It's like you rip them out, put them somewhere else and forget about it. I think it's important that the kids do know they are going someplace else. Also, maybe the kids think, "Maybe Betty didn't want him anymore." Maybe the day before I happened to say to him, "You can't do those kinds of things!" And maybe those kids believe that he did something bad so he cannot come here again.

I wish sometimes somebody would call me up and say, "Look I'm going to kill that kid if I can't talk to somebody." . . . Even I had that feeling when my daughter was real small and was going through the thing where she couldn't sleep at night. There were many times I remember sitting in bed having the pillow over my head saying, "Please god, help me. I can't take it anymore." I had the exact same feelings. But then you pull yourself together and you pick up your kid and if she cries 3 more hours you walk up and down the halls. I think everybody who has kids has had that feeling.

Maybe because of my being adopted, maybe there is something there, that you try to . . . prevent them from getting hurt. . . . As a child it really does bother you. The only thing I could think of was "What was the matter with me?" You see all those cute babies. Who doesn't love a baby? What did I do? Did I scream too much? . . . when I met my real brother, he feels the same way. . . . He said all his life he has had kids around. . . .

I tried other stuff. I went to hairdresser school. I even worked in a factory. I made great money. I've been doing this for the longest time now and I enjoy it. Maybe there is a time when you have to do something else for a while. I'm trying to do stuff after work.

My husband has a different shift. He is glad when he comes home. He likes to stay at home. Me, I'm cooped up in the house. I want to get out. Now we do one weekend with the kids and one weekend we do something [together]. He works in a jail. We sit together. He tells me about the jail. I tell him about day care. We both look at each other and say, "We're crazy. Let's do something. Let's get away." (Sheehan, 1989)

References

Alldred, P., & Gillies, V. (2002). Eliciting research accounts: Re\producing modern subjects. In M. Mauthner, M. Birch, J. Jessop, & T. Miller (Eds.), *Ethics in qualitative research* (pp. 91–106). London: Sage.

American Anthropological Association. (1983). *Professional ethics: Standards and procedures of the American Anthropological Association.* Washington, DC: Author.

American Humane Fact Sheet. (Accessed April 18, 2005). *http:\\american humane. org\site\DocServer\nr_Factsheet_Reporting.PDF?docid-1274*

Anderson, B. A., Silver, B. D., & Abramson, P. R. (1988). The effects of the race of the interviewer on race related attitudes of black respondents in SRC\ CPS national election studies. *Public Opinion Quarterly, 52,* 289–324.

Anderson, P. V. (1996). Ethics, institutional review boards, and the involvement of human participants in composition research. In P. Mortensen & G. E. Kirsch (Eds.), *Ethical representation in qualitative studies of literacy* (pp. 260–285). Urbana, IL: National Council of Teachers of English.

Annas, G. (1992). The changing landscape of human experimentation: Nuremberg, Helsinki and beyond. *Health Matrix: The Journal of Law-Medicine, 2,* 119–140.

Applebaum, P. S., Lidz, C. W., & Meisel, A. (1987). *Informed consent: Legal practice and theory.* New York: Oxford University Press.

Aristotle. (1976). *The ethics of Aristotle: The Nicomachean ethics* (J. A. K. Thomson, Trans.). London: Penguin.

Bailyn, B. (1963). Education as a discipline. In J. Walton & J. L. Luwethe (Eds.), *The discipline of education* (pp. 126–129). Madison: University of Wisconsin Press.

Becker, H. S., & Geer, B. (1957). Participant observation and interviewing: A comparison. *Human Organization, 16*(3), 28–32.

Bell, L., & Nutt, L. (2002). Divided loyalties, divided expectations: Research ethics, professional and occupational responsibilities. In M. Mauthner, M. Birch, J. Jessop, & T. Miller (Eds.), *Ethics in qualitative research* (pp. 70–90). London: Sage.

Bernard, H. R. (1994). *Research methods in anthropology* (2nd ed.). Thousand Oaks, CA: Sage.

Bernstein, B. (1975). *Class, codes and control: Vol. 3. Towards a theory of educational transmission.* London: Routledge and Kegan Paul.

Bertaux, D. (Ed.). (1981). *Biography and society: The life history approach in the social sciences.* Beverly Hills, CA: Sage.

Birch, M., & Miller, T. (2002). Encouraging participation, ethics and responsibilities. In M. Mauthner, M. Birch, J. Jessop, & T. Miller (Eds.), *Ethics in qualitative research* (pp. 91–106). London: Sage.

Blauner, B. (1987). Problems of editing "first-person" sociology. *Qualitative Sociology, 10*(1), pp. 46–64.

Blumer, H. (1969). *Symbolic interactionism: Perspective and method.* Englewood Cliffs, NJ: Prentice Hall.

Bogdan, R., & Taylor, S. J. (1975). *Introduction to research methods: A phenomenological approach to the social sciences.* New York: Wiley.

Boushel, M. (2000). What kind of people are we? "Race," anti-racism and social welfare research. *British Journal of Social Work, 30,* 71–89.

Brannen, J. (1988). Research note: The study of sensitive subjects. *Sociological Review, 36*(3), 552–563.

Brenner, M., Brown, J., & Canter, D. (Eds.). (1985). *The research interview: Uses and approaches.* London: Academic Press.

Briggs, C. L. (1986). *Learning how to ask: A sociolinguistic appraisal of the role of the interview in social science research.* Cambridge, England: Cambridge University Press.

Bronowski, J. (Narrator). (1973). *Ascent of Man: Knowledge of Certainty, #11* [Film]. Paramus, NJ: Time Life Video.

Brooks, J. (2005, April 15). *Current and emerging issues in human subjects research.* Presentation at Second Annual Conference on Ethics in Graduate Education, University of Massachsuetts Amherst.

Bruner, J. (1996). *The culture of education.* Cambridge, MA: Harvard University Press.

Burke, K. (1990). *The experience of communications majors.* Unpublished manuscript, University of Massachusetts, Amherst.

Bury, J. B. (1932). *The idea of progress.* New York: Dover.

Butcher, S. H. (Ed. and Trans.). (1902). *The poetics of Aristotle.* London: MacMillan.

Callaway, H. (1981). Women's perspective: Research as revision. In P. Reason & J. Rowan (Eds.), *Human inquiry* (pp. 457–471). New York: Wiley.

Campbell, D., & Stanley, J. (1963). Experimental and quasi-experimental design for research in teaching. In N. L. Gage (Ed.), *Handbook of research on teaching* (pp. 171–246). Chicago: Rand McNally.

Carlisle, L. (1988). Response to literature among first graders: Exploring the possibilities. *Comprehensive Dissertation Index 1988,* DEV88-13203.

Cassell, J. (1978). Risk and benefit to subjects of fieldwork. *The American Sociologist, 13,* 134–143.

Charmaz, K. (1983). The grounded theory method: An explication and interpretation. In R. Emerson (Ed.), *Contemporary field research: A collection of readings* (pp. 109–126). Boston: Little Brown.

Charmaz, K. (1991). Translating graduate qualitative methods into undergraduate teaching: Intensive interviewing as a case example. *Teaching Sociology, 19*(3), 384–395.

Cleary, L. M. (1985). *The experience of 11th grade writers: The interaction of thought and emotion in the writing process.* Unpublished doctoral dissertation, University of Massachusetts, Amherst.

Cleary, L. M. (1988). A profile of Carlos: Strengths of a non-standard dialect writer. *English Journal, 77*(1), 59–64.

Cleary, L. M. (1990). The fragile inclination to write: Praise and criticism in the classroom. *English Journal, 79*(2), 22–28.

Cleary, L. M. (1991). *From the other side of the desk: Students speak out about writing.* Portsmouth, NH: Boynton\Cook.

Cleary, L. M. (2005, March 31). *Research in progress: The ethics of cross cultural research in educational settings: More questions than answers.* Presentation at Forum Series on the Ethics of Person-Based Research, sponsored by the Graduate School, University of Massachusetts, Amherst.

Cleary, L. M., & Peacock, T. (1997). *Collected wisdom: American Indian education.* Boston: Allyn and Bacon.

Code of Federal Regulations (2001). Title 45 Public Welfare, Part 46 Protection of Human Subjects. Washington, DC: United States Department of Health and Human Services.

Compagnone, W. (1995). *Student teachers in urban high schools: An interview study of neophytes in neverland.* Unpublished doctoral dissertation, University of Massachusetts, Amherst.

Conkright, S. L. (1997). *Personal adoption of the fundamental nature of participatory leadership: An interview study of the transformation of elites' business practice.* Unpublished doctoral dissertation, George Washington University, Washington, DC

Cook, J. (2004) *Coming into my own as a teacher: English teachers' experience in their first year of teaching.* Unpublished doctoral dissertation, University of Massachusetts, Amherst.

Corbin, J., & Morse, J. M. (2003). The unstructured interactive interview: Issues of reciprocity and risks when dealing with sensitive topics. *Qualitative Inquiry, 9*(3), 335–354.

Cotter, P. R., Cohen, J., & Coulter, P. B. (1982). Race-of-interviewer effects in telephone interviews. *Public Opinion Quarterly, 46,* 278–283.

Davis, J. (1984). Data into text. In R. F. Ellen (Ed.), *Ethnographic research: A guide to general conduct* (pp. 295–318). London: Academic Press.

Dean, J. P., & Whyte, W. F. (1958). How do you know the informant is telling the truth? *Human Organization, 17*(2), 34–38.

de Laine, M. (2000). *Fieldwork, participation and practice: Ethics and dilemmas in qualitative research.* London: Sage.

Devault, M. L. (1990). Talking and listening from women's standpoint: Feminist strategies for interviewing and analysis. *Social Problems, 37*(1), 96–116.

Dexter, L. A. (1970). *Elite and specialized interviewing.* Evanston, IL: Northwestern University Press.

Dey, I. (1993). *Qualitative data analysis: A user-friendly guide for social scientists.* London: Routledge.

Dollard, J. (1949). *Caste and class in a southern town.* Garden City, NY: Doubleday Anchor Books.

Douglas, J. (1976). *Investigative social research: Individual and team field research.* Beverly Hills, CA: Sage.

Douglas, J. (1979). Living morality versus bureaucratic fiat. In C. B. Klockars & F. W. O'Connor (Eds.), *Deviance and decency* (pp. 13–34). Beverly Hills, CA: Sage.

Douglas, J. (1985). *Creative interviewing.* Beverly Hills, CA: Sage.

Dyson, F. (2004). One in a million. [Review of the book *Debunked! Esp, telekinesis, other pseudoscience.*] *New York Review of Books, LI,* 5, 5.

Education Sciences Reform Act of 2002. (2002). 20 United States Code Service 9501.

Edwards, R. (1990). Connecting methods and epistemology: A White woman interviewing Black women. *Women's Studies International Forum, 13*(5), 477–490.

Elbow, P. (1981). *Writing with power.* Oxford, England: Oxford University Press.

Ellen, R. F. (Ed.). (1984). *Ethnographic research: A guide to general conduct.* London: Academic Press.

Elliott-Johns, S. (2004). *Theoretical orientations to reading and instructional practices of eleven grade five teachers.* Unpublished doctoral dissertation, McGill University, Montreal.

Faden, R. B., & Beauchamp, T. L. (1986). *A history and theory of informed consent.* New York: Oxford University Press.

Fay, B. (1987). *Critical social science: Liberation and its limits.* Ithaca, NY: Cornell University Press.

Ferrarotti, F. (1981). On the autonomy of the biographical method. In D. Bertaux (Ed.), *Biography and society: The life history approach in the social sciences* (pp. 19–27). Beverly Hills, CA: Sage.

Fischetti, J. C., Santilli, S. A., & Seidman, I. E. (1988). *The mask of teacher education reform.* Unpublished manuscript, University of Massachusetts, Amherst.

Fish, S. (1980). *Is there a text in this class?* Cambridge, MA: Harvard University Press.

Frank, N. (2000). *The experience of six mainland Chinese women in American graduate programs.* Unpublished doctoral dissertation, University of Denver, Colorado.

Frenzy at UMass. (1970, December 21). *Time,* p. 34.

Fuderich, T. (1995). *The psychology of children of war.* Unpublished manuscript, University of Massachusetts, Amherst.

Gabriel, J. (1997). *The experiences of language minority students in mainstream English classes in United States public high schools: A study through in-depth interviewing.* Unpublished doctoral dissertation, University of Massachusetts, Amherst.

Gage, N. L. (Ed.). (1963). *Handbook of research on teaching.* Chicago: Rand McNally.

Gage, N. L. (1989). The paradigm wars and their aftermath: A "historical" sketch of research on teaching. *Educational Researcher, 18*(7), 4–10.

Galvan, S. (1990). *Experience of minority teachers in local teachers union.* Unpublished manuscript, University of Massachusetts, Amherst.

Garman, N. (1994). Qualitative inquiry: Meaning and menace for educational researchers. In J. S. Smyth (Ed.), *Conference proceedings for the mini-conference, Qualitative Approaches in Educational Research*. Flinders University, South Australia, pp. 3–12.

Gergen, K. J. (2001). Foreword. In S. Wortham, *Narratives in action: A strategy for research and analysis*. New York: Teachers College Press.

Gitlin, T. (1987). *The sixties: Years of hope, days of rage*. New York: Bantam Books.

Glaser, B. G., & Strauss, A. S. (1967). *The discovery of grounded theory: Strategies for qualitative research*. New York: Aldine De Gruyter.

Goldstein, T. (1995). Interviewing in a multicultural\multilingual setting. *TESOL Quarterly, 29*(39), 587–593.

Gordon, R. (1987). *Interviewing strategies*. Chicago: Dorsey Press.

Gove, P. B. (Ed.). (1971). *Webster's third new international dictionary of the English language, unabridged*. Springfield, MA: G & C Merriam.

Griffin, P. (1989, March 28). *Using participant research to empower gay and lesbian educators*. Paper presented at the American Educational Research Association Annual Conference, San Francisco, CA.

Hardin, C. (1987). Black professional musicians in higher education: A dissertation based on in-depth interviews. *Comprehensive Dissertation Index 1983–1987*, DEU87–10458.

Heller, J. (1972, July 26). Syphilis victims in U.S. study went untreated for 40 years. *New York Times*, p. 1.

Herod, A. (1993). Gender issues in the use of interviewing as a research method. *Professional Geographer, 45*(3), 305–316.

Heron, J. (1981). The philosophical basis for a new paradigm. In P. Reason & J. Rowan (Eds.), *Human inquiry* (pp. 19–35). New York: Wiley.

Hertz, R., & Imber, J. B. (Eds.). (1995). *Studying elites using qualitative methods*. Thousand Oaks, CA: Sage.

Hirsch, A. (1982). Copyrighting conversations: Applying the 1976 copyright act to interviews. *American University Law Review, 31*, 1071–1093.

Hubbell, L. D. (2003). False starts, suspicious interviewees and nearly impossible tasks: Some reflections on the difficulty of conducting field research abroad. *The Qualitative Report, 8*(2), 195–209.

Hyman, H. H., Cobb, W. J., Fledman, J. J., Hart, C. W., & Stember, C. H. (1954). *Interviewing in social research*. Chicago: University of Chicago Press.

James, W. (1947). *Essays in radical empiricism* and *In a pluralistic universe*. New York: Longmans, Green.

Jenoure, T. (1995). *Navigators, challengers, dreamers: African American musicians, dancers, and visual artists who teach at traditionally white colleges and universities*. Unpublished doctoral dissertation, University of Massachusetts, Amherst.

Johnson, J. (1975). *Doing field research*. New York: Free Press.

Kahn, R. L., & Cannell, C. F. (1960). *The dynamics of interviewing*. New York: Wiley.

Kanter, R. M. (1977). *Men and women of the corporation*. New York: Basic Books.

Kelman, H. C. (1977). Privacy and research with human beings. *Journal of Social Issues, 33*(3), 169–195.

Kirsch, G. (1999). *Ethical dilemmas in feminist research: The politics of location, interpretation, and publication.* Albany: State University of New York Press.

Kolata, G. (2001, July 17). Johns Hopkins admits fault in fatal experiment. *New York Times,* p. 16.

Kuhn, T. S. (1970). *The structure of scientific revolution* (2nd ed.). Chicago: University of Chicago Press.

Kuhn, S. (1996). Unpublished syllabus, College of Management, University of Massachusetts, Lowell.

Kvale, S. (1996). *Interviews: An introduction to qualitative research interviewing.* Thousand Oaks, CA: Sage.

Labov, W. (1972). Logic of non-standard English. In *Language in the inner city: Studies in Black English vernacular* (pp. 201–240). Philadelphia: University of Pennsylvania Press.

Lather, P. (1986a). Issues of validity in open ideological research: Between a rock and a soft place. *Interchange, 17*(4), 63–84.

Lather, P. (1986b). Research as praxis. *Harvard Educational Review, 56*(3), 257–277.

Lee, R. M. (1993). *Doing research on sensitive topics.* London: Sage.

Liberman, K. (1999). From walkabout to meditation: Craft and ethics in field inquiry. *Qualitative Inquiry, 5,* 547–563.

Lightfoot, S. L. (1983). *The good high school: Portraits of character and culture.* New York: Basic Books.

Lincoln, Y. S., & Guba, E. G. (1985). *Naturalistic inquiry.* Beverly Hills, CA: Sage.

Locke, L. (1989). Qualitative research as a form of scientific inquiry in sport and physical education. *Research Quarterly for Exercise and Sport, 60*(1), 1–20.

Locke, L. F., Spirduso, W., & Silverman, S. J. (2000). *Proposals that work: A guide for planning dissertations and grants proposals* (4th ed.). Beverly Hills, CA: Sage.

Locke, L. F., Silverman, S. J., and Spirduso, W. (2004). *Reading and understanding research,* (2nd ed.). Thousand Oaks, CA: Sage.

Lofland, J. (1971). *Analyzing social settings.* Belmont, CA: Wadsworth.

Lynch, D. J. S. (1997). *Among advisors: An interview study of advising at a public, land grant university.* Unpublished doctoral dissertation. University of Massachusetts, Amherst.

Macur, J. (2005, April 15). Standing up after fearing standing out. *New York Times,* p. C14.

Mannheim, K. (1975). *Ideology and utopia.* New York: Free Press.

Marshall, C., & Rossman, G. B. (1989). *Designing qualitative research.* Newbury Park, CA: Sage.

Marshall, J. (1981). Making sense as a personal process. In P. Reason & J. Rowan (Eds.), *Human inquiry* (pp. 395–399). New York: Wiley.

Matson, F. (1966). *The broken image: Man, science, and society.* Garden City, NY: Archer Books.

Mattingly, C. (1998). *Healing dramas and clinical plots: The narrative structure of experience.* Cambridge, England: Cambridge University Press.

Maxwell, J. A. (1996). *Qualitative research design: An interpretive approach.* Thousand Oaks, CA: Sage.

McKee, H. (2004). Statement at University of Massachusetts Sociology Department Forum on Ethics and the Social Sciences, October 1, 2004.

McCracken, G. (1988). *The long interview.* Beverly Hills, CA: Sage.

McLuhan, M. (1965). *Understanding media: The extensions of man.* New York: McGraw-Hill.

Miles, M. B., & Huberman, A. M. (1984). *Qualitative data analysis: A sourcebook of new methods.* Beverly Hills, CA: Sage.

Miller, J. H. (1993). *Gender issues embedded in the experience of women student teachers: A study using in-depth interviews.* Unpublished doctoral dissertation, University of Massachusetts, Amherst.

Miller, J. H. (1997). Gender issues embedded in the experience of student teaching: Being treated like a sex object. *Journal of Teacher Education, 48*(1), 19–28.

Mishler, E. G. (1979). Meaning in context: Is there any other kind? *Harvard Educational Review, 49*(1), 1–19.

Mishler, E. G. (1986). *Research interviewing.* Cambridge, MA: Harvard University Press.

Mishler, E. G. (1991). Representing discourse: The rhetoric of transcription. *Journal of Narrative and Life History, 1*(4), 255–280.

Mitchell, R. G., Jr. (1993). *Secrecy and fieldwork.* Newbury Park, CA: Sage.

Mitscherlich, A., & Mielke, F. (1949). *Doctors of infamy: The story of Nazi medical crimes* (H. Norden, Trans.). New York: Henry Schuman.

Morse, J. M. (1994). Emerging from the data: The cognitive process of analysis in qualitative inquiry. In J. Morse (Ed.), *Critical issues in qualitative research methods* (pp. 23–43). Thousand Oaks, CA: Sage.

Mostyn, B. (1985). The content analysis of qualitative research data: A dynamic approach. In M. Brenner, J. Brown, & D. Canter (Eds.), *The research interview: Uses and approaches* (pp. 115–145). London: Academic Press.

Moustakas, C. (1994). *Phenomenological research methods.* Thousand Oaks, CA: Sage.

Nagle, J. (1995). *Voices from the margins: A phenomenological interview study of twenty vocational high school students' educational histories.* Unpublished doctoral dissertation, University of Massachusetts, Amherst.

Nagle, J. (2001). *Voices from the margins: The stories of vocational high school students.* New York: Peter Lang.

The National Commission for the Protection of Human Subjects of Biomedical and Behavioral Research. (1979). *Belmont report: Ethical principles and guidelines for the protection of human subjects of research.* Washington, DC: Department of Health and Human Services.

Nejelski, P., & Lerman, L. M. (1971). A researcher-subject testimonial privilege: What to do before the subpoena arrives. *Wisconsin Law Review, 1085*(4), 1084–1148.

Oakley, A. (1981). Interviewing women: A contradiction in terms. In H. Roberts (Ed.), *Doing feminist research* (pp. 30–61). Boston: Routledge and Kegan Paul.

O'Donnell, J. F. (1990). *Tracking: Its socializing impact on student teachers: A qualitative study using in-depth phenomenological interviewing.* Unpublished doctoral dissertation, University of Massachusetts, Amherst.

O'Donnell, J. F., Schneider, H., Seidman, I. E., & Tingitana, A. (1989, March 2–5). *The complexities of teacher education in a professional development school: A study through in-depth interviews.* Paper presented at annual meeting of the American Association of Teacher Education, Anaheim, CA. (ERIC Document Reproduction Service No. ED 309 153).

O'Neil, R. M. (1996). A researcher's privilege: Does any hope remain. *Law and Contemporary Problems, 59*(3), 35–49.

Oral History Association. (1992). *Oral History Association evaluation guidelines.* Los Angeles: Author.

Oral History Association. (Accessed July 8, 2005). *Oral history excluded from IRB review. http:\\omega.dickinson.edu\organizations\oha*

Parker, T. (1996). *Studs Terkel: A life in words.* New York: Henry Holt.

Patai, D. (1987). Ethical problems of personal narratives, or, who should eat the last piece of cake? *International Journal of Oral History, 8*(1), 5–27.

Patai, D. (1988). *Brazilian women speak: Contemporary life stories.* [Interviews edited and translated by Daphne Patai]. New Brunswick, NJ: Rutgers University Press.

Patton, M. Q. (1989). *Qualitative evaluation methods* (10th printing). Beverly Hills, CA: Sage.

Phoenix, A. (1994). Practicing feminist research: The *intersection* of gender and "race" in the research process. In M. Maynard & J. Purvis, *Researching women's lives from a feminist perspective* (pp. 49–71). London: Taylor and Francis.

Polanyi, M. (1958). *Personal knowledge.* Chicago: University of Chicago Press.

Popkowitz, T. S. (1984). *Paradigm and ideology in educational research.* London: Falmer Press.

Protection of Human Subjects. (2001). 45 C.F.R sections 46.101-46.409 (2001).

Reason, P. (1981). Methodological approaches to social science. In P. Reason & J. Rowan (Eds.), *Human inquiry* (pp. 43–51). New York: Wiley.

Reason, P. (Ed.). (1994). *Participation in human inquiry.* London: Sage.

Reese, S. D., Danielson, W. A., Shoemaker, P. J., Chang, T. K., & Hsu, H-L. (1986). Ethnicity of interviewer effects among Mexican Americans and Anglos. *Public Opinion Quarterly, 50,* 563–573.

Resnik, H. (1972, March 4). Are there better ways to teach teachers? *Saturday Review,* pp. 46–50.

Reynolds, P. D. (1979). *Ethical dilemmas and social science research.* San Francisco: Jossey-Bass.

Richardson, S. A., Dohrenwend, B. S., & Klein, D. (1965). *Interviewing: Its forms and functions.* New York: Basic Books.

Riessman, C. K. (1987). When gender is not enough: Women interviewing women. *Gender and Society, 1*(2), 172–207.

Ritchie, D. A. (2003). *Doing oral history: A practical guide*. New York: Oxford University Press.

Rosenblatt, L. (1982). The literary translation: Evocation and response. *Theory Into Practice, 21*(4), 268–277.

Rosser, S. V. (1992). Are there feminist methodologies appropriate for the natural sciences and do they make a difference? *Women's Studies International Forum, 15*(5\6), 535–550.

Rowan, J. (1981). A dialectical paradigm for research. In P. Reason & J. Rowan (Eds.), *Human inquiry* (pp. 93–112). New York: Wiley.

Rowe, M. B. (1974). The relationship of wait-time and rewards to the development of language, logic, and fate control: Part II–Rewards. *Journal of research in science teaching, 11*(4), 291–308.

Rubin, H. J., & Rubin, I. S. (1995). *Qualitative interviewing: The art of hearing*. Thousand Oaks, CA: Sage.

Sartre, J. P. (1968). *Search for a method* (H. E. Barnes, Trans.). New York: Random House.

Schatzkamer, M. B. (1986). Returning women students in the community college: A feminist perspective. *Comprehensive Dissertation Index 1983–1987*, DEU87–01215.

Schram, T. H. (2003). *Conceptualizing qualitative inquiry: mindwork for fieldwork in education*. Upper Saddle River, NJ: Merrill\Prentice Hall.

Schuman, D. (1982). *Policy analysis, education, and everyday life*. Lexington, MA: Heath.

Schutz, A. (1967). *The phenomenology of the social world* (G. Walsh & F. Lenhert, Trans.). Chicago: Northwestern University Press.

Seidman, E. (1985). *In the words of the faculty: Perspectives on improving teaching and educational quality in community colleges*. San Francisco: Jossey-Bass.

Seidman, E., Sullivan, P., & Schatzkamer, M. (1983). *The work of community college faculty: A study through in-depth interviews* (Final Report to the National Institute of Education). Washington, DC. (ERIC Document Reproduction Service No. ED 243 499).

Sennett, R., & Cobb, J. (1972). *The hidden injuries of class*. New York: Knopf.

Shavelson, R. J., & Towne, L. (Eds.). (2002). *Scientific research in education*. Washington, DC: National Academy Press.

Sheehan, M. (1989). *Child care as a career: A study of long term child care providers*. Unpublished manuscript, University of Massachusetts, Amherst.

Shils, E. A. (1959). Social inquiry and the autonomy of the individual. In D. Lerner (Ed.), *The human meaning of the social science* (pp. 114–157). Cleveland, OH: Meridian Books.

Smith, L. (1992). Ethical issues in interviewing. *Journal of Advanced Nursing, 17*, 98–103.

Solsken, J. (1989, May 3). *Micro-macro: A critical ethnographic perspective on classroom reading and writing as a social process*. Remarks presented at the annual meeting of the International Reading Association, New Orleans, LA.

Song, M., & Parker, D. (1995). Commonality, difference and the dynamics of disclosure in in-depth interviewing. *Sociology, 29*(2), 241–256.

Spradley, J. P. (1979). *The ethnographic interview.* New York: Holt, Rinehart, and Winston.

Stacey, J. (1988). Can there be a feminist ethnography? *Women's Studies International Forum, 2*(1), 21–27.

Steiner, G. (1978). The distribution of discourse. In G. Steiner, *On difficulty and other essays* (pp. 61–94). New York: Oxford University Press.

Stolberg, S. G. (2000, January 27). Teenager's death is shaking up field of human gene therapy. *New York Times,* p. 20.

Sullivan, P. (Producer\Director), & Seidman, I. E. (Co-director). (1982). *In their own words: Working in the community college* [Film]. Amherst: University of Massachusetts.

Sullivan, P. (Producer\Director), & Speidel, J. (Producer\Director). (1976). *The Shaker legacy* [Film]. Amherst: University of Massachusetts.

Tagg, S. K. (1985). Life story interviews and their interpretations. In M. Brenner, J. Brown, & D. Canter (Eds.), *The research interview: Uses and approaches* (pp. 163–199). London: Academic Press.

Terkel, S. (1972). *Working.* New York: Pantheon Books.

Thelen, D. (1989, September 27). A new approach to understanding human memory offers a solution to the crisis in the study of history. *The Chronicle of Higher Education,* pp. B1, B3.

Thorne, B. (1980). "You still takin' notes?" Fieldwork and problems of informed consent. *Social Problems, 27*(3), 284–297.

Todorov, T. (1984). *The conquest of America* (R. Howard, Trans.). New York: Harper and Row. (Original work published 1982)

Tremblay, B. (1990). *The experience of instructional design.* Unpublished manuscript, University of Massachusetts, Amherst.

Trow, M. (1957). Comment on "Participant observation and interviewing: A comparison." *Human Organization, 16*(3), 33–35.

University of New Hampshire. (2004). *Information individuals in New Hampshire are legally required to report.* Durham, NH: Office of Sponsored Research–Research-Research Conduct and Compliance Services.

Van Manen, M. (1990). *Researching lived experience: Human science for an action sensitive pedagogy.* London, Canada: The University of Western Ontario.

Vygotsky, L. (1987). *Thought and language* (A. Kozulin, Ed.). Cambridge, MA: MIT Press.

Watkins, C. (Ed.). (1985). *The American heritage dictionary of Indo-European roots.* Boston: Houghton Mifflin.

Weiss, R. S. (1994). *Learning from strangers: The art and method of qualitative interview studies.* New York: The Free Press.

Whiting, G. W. (2004). *Young Black fathers in a fatherhood program: A phenomenological study.* Unpublished doctoral dissertation, Purdue University, West Lafayette, IN.

Wideman, J. E. (1990). Introduction to *The souls of black folk* by W. E. B. Du Bois. New York: Random House.

Williams, C. L., & Heikes, E. J. (1993). The importance of researcher's gender in the in-depth interview: Evidence from two case studies of male nurses. *Gender and Society, 7*(2), 280–291.

Williamson, K. (1988). *A phenomenological description of the professional lives and experiences of physical education teacher educators.* Unpublished doctoral dissertation, University of Massachusetts, Amherst.

Williamson, K. (1990). The ivory tower: Myth or reality. *Journal of Teaching in Physical Education, 9*(2), 95–105.

Wolcott, H. F. (1990). *Writing up qualitative research.* Newbury Park, CA: Sage.

Wolcott, H. F. (1994). *Transforming qualitative data.* Thousand Oaks, CA: Sage.

Woods, S. (1990). *The contextual realities of being a lesbian physical educator: Living in two worlds.* Unpublished doctoral dissertation, University of Massachusetts, Amherst.

Young, E. H., & Lee, R. (1996). Fieldworker feelings as data: "Emotion work" and "feeling rules" in first person accounts of sociological fieldwork. In V. James & J. Gabe (Eds.), *Health and the sociology of emotions* (pp. 97–113). Oxford, England: Blackwell.

Young, S. (1990). *ESL teachers and their work—A study based on interviews conducted with teachers of English as a second language.* Unpublished doctoral dissertation, University of Massachusetts, Amherst.

Yow, V. R. (1994). *Recording oral history: A practical guide for social scientists.* Thousand Oaks, CA: Sage.

Index

About the Author

Irving Seidman is a professor of qualitative research and secondary teacher education at the School of Education, University of Massachusetts, Amherst. He is the author of *Oswald Tippo and the Early Promise of the University of Massachusetts* (2002), *The Essential Career Guide to Becoming a Middle and High School Teacher* with Robert Maloy (1999), *In the Words of the Faculty* (1985), and articles published under the name Earl Seidman.